PROPHET MUHAMMAD: THE GREATEST BENEFACTOR

PROPHET MUHAMMAD
THE GREATEST BENEFACTOR

By
Satish Ganjoo

ANMOL PUBLICATIONS PVT. LTD.
NEW DELHI - 110 002 (INDIA)

ANMOL PUBLICATIONS PVT. LTD.
4374/4B, Ansari Road, Daryaganj
New Delhi - 110 002
Ph.: 23261597, 23278000
Visit us at: www.anmolpublications.com

Prophet Muhammad: The Greatest Benefactor

First Published, 2004

ISBN 81-261-1421-5

PRINTED IN INDIA

Published by J.L. Kumar for Anmol Publications Pvt. Ltd., New Delhi - 110 002 and Printed at Mehra Offset Press, Delhi.

Contents

PREFACE

"There is no god but One God, and Muhammad is His Prophet," is the starting and basic point of all his teachings. Undisputably, in the history of World the Holy Prophet is regarded as the greatest of all benefactors.

Before the advent of the Prophet, the world was in a perilous state, but he changed everything, making all human beings equal and ending once and for all the questions of superiority and inferiority. The Holy Prophet dedicated his life to preaching the world of God with such wisdom and resolution of purpose that it is difficult to separate him from the attributes of God, and because of this he has attained to such a perfection of humanity that he is, and always will be, the greatest benefactor of the world.

In the present anthology we have chosen thirteen articles, penned by great scholars of religion and theology which were originally published in various Journals of great reputation, in different issues.

A collection of articles, or an anthology, has many benefits, like, it renews our acquaintance with the literature we have neglected, it reveals to us material of which we were ignorant, and it exposes relationship where we did not suppose them to exist.

A word of acknowledgement is due to the inspiration of the idea of a comprehensive, cumulative and compact compilation of articles on the Holy Prophet, his life, teachings, and some vital issues pertaining to his life. These inspirers are from all walks of life and their efforts must be acknowledged which includes contributors, authors and editors, as well as the publishers and copyright holders who have graciously contributed to this work and we duly acknowledge their cooperation.

The well wishers are many more and listing of all the concerned by names is impossible here. Each must be duly rewarded for his gesture and this is our sincere prayer to Allah, the Almighty.

—Editor

1

Muhammad: The World's Greatest Benefactor

In the history of the world the Holy Prophet is regarded as the greatest of all benefactors, and this is a fact that even the greatest commentator has to acknowledge. The starting and basic point of all his teachings is that "there is no god but One God, and Muhammad is His Prophet."

The history of the world shows that from the time of the first religious person to the beginning of the new civilization the world has remained divided between two groups of people, the oppressor and the oppressed. One assumed superiority over the other; difference of birth, race and wealth, pomp and power made it regard the other with contempt. The trouble to-day is the same; there is everlastingly some dispute over Imperialism, colour and race. And there are disputes between the rich and the poor, the employer and the employed, the landlord and the peasant, and the like, for self-delusion and self-aggrandisement are still the cause, as they always were, of all human troubles and misunderstandings.

The only remedy for this state of things is the Book which Allah revealed to the Holy Prophet 1300 years ago. This book is so complete and sufficient, both as regards its language and spirit, that in spite of all the advance made in modern thought the greatest thinkers of to-day cannot say a world against it. This book is so simple that it needs no priests to interpret it to the Muslims. It is so great a book, that it is no wonder that a hardened critic like Professor D. S. Margoliouth was obliged, in the preface of the Qur-án, by Rodwell, to admit its greatness. The Qur-án, by its perfect teachings, has induced the Muslims to make themselves masters of all the sciences and arts of the world, with the result that Islam became the University of Europe in the Middle Ages. Before the Prophet's advent the world was in a perilous state, but he changed everything, making all human beings equal and ending once and for all the questions of superiority and inferiority.

Not only did he make an end of slavery, but he repudiated all such ideas and notions as make one man despise another. It is the teachings of the Prophet that have given us our democratic institutions wherein the King rules by and with the advice and consent of the representatives of the people. This teaches us to respect the opinion of another person, and thus a spirit is born which guides us to solve all the hidden problems of humanity. And so the prophet established a brotherhood which knows no restrictions of colour, race, wealth and power and under which all stand shoulder to shoulder to pray to the One and only God Who is True and Real.

He taught us that birth was an event over which human beings had no control. Wealth, he said, cannot be attained without the help of others and asked men to keep "zakat" (poor-rate) separate as a way of co-operation with others. Strength, he said, was the result of natural and physical conditions. The education of the heart depends on self-exertion. "The heart of mankind is the science of wisdom; it leads a man either to Hell or Heaven."

Mr. H. G. Wells, the famous author of to-day writes: "Muhammad was not a liar... his thoughts used to be the same as God's revelation." No doubt the Holy prophet dedicated his life to preaching the word of God with such wisdom and resolution of purpose that it is difficult to separate him from the attributes of God, and because of this he has attained to such a perfection of humanity that he is, and always will be, the greatest benefactor of the world.

I think it is a pity that the world to-day puts things of no worth before that which alone can bring love and peace to humanity. It is high time that we realized that World Peace and harmonious international relations can only be achieved in following the "principles of Islam." A time surely will come, sooner or later, when the world will be forced to admit that the only means to end all its troubles is to follow the perfect teachings and examples of the Holy Prophet, writes Mr. George Bernard Shaw in his "Getting Married."

From time to time Allah sent prophets for the reform and guidance of the people, and to bring to life their deadened feelings by stirring in them a desire for spiritual attainment. Every Prophet came with this mission. They were all builders of spirituality, and they discharged their duties with honour and credit, and succeeded in their efforts. It is, of course, a different thing that later generations regarded their teachings as wrong, or interpreted them wrongly; but it remains a truth and a fact that these Prophets were all messengers of One and the same God, and the preachers of the highest form of spirituality. They succeeded in leading the poor wanderers back to the true path, for only those who came from God can reform others and guide them back to god. Spirituality was the combined mission of all Prophets and the sole purpose of the creation of man.

All religious teachers are equally agreed on the importance of the attainment of spirituality, and have made it the foundation of their respective religions, but their followers differed always in their concepts of the word. Some understood it to be the renunciation of the world, and the severance of all human connections; others made celibacy the means for its attainment. Some regarded the abstinence from delicious food and fine clothing to be spirituality; others the saying of prayers without end, the performance of all sorts of rituals, litanies and the like. Many and varied definitions have made of the word a mystery. All were eager for it, but none were agreed over the meaning of it. The Holy Prophet Muhammad, at his coming, taught them all that their conceptions of spirituality were entirely wrong: he taught and made them believe that spirituality is something above and beyond all religious practices.

The falsity of their conceptions becomes clear when it is pointed out that God would not have created so many things in the world, if he had wished human beings to abstain from or renounce them. The very fact that God has created such things is enough to show that He desired human beings to participate in them, and—who knows—by their aid to attain to spirituality. I should say that the participation in all things created, except in things forbidden, is essential for the attainment of spirituality; to renounce them is wrong, and an act of sheer ingratitude to God. That is why those who followed the former policy have failed hopelessly in the attainment of spirituality. True spirituality consists of the method adopted, together with participation in the things created. Allah sent man after showing him the difference between Right and Wrong, to adopt a course in practical life that would lead him back to Him. If there was no wrong in the world, the right and goodness become nothing, and less than nothing. Spirituality is not to renounce the world in order to avoid wrong and attain good. Wrong should not be shunned, but fought with resolution and courage. True spirituality is, to remain in the human world, amidst all temptations; then to combat all evil and attain good. If a blind man says he is good because he has never seen any one of the opposite sex with lust, then he is wrong, he did not look because he could not see; probably, had he had sight, he would have looked; but to have eyes and then not to look with lust would be good. Similarly, those who renounce the world cannot say that they are really good, for they shut themselves up in solitude, away from all worldly temptation, so that they cannot help being good. The beauty and greatness of what is good and what is right lie in the presence of their opposite qualities; then they become valuable. A person can only hope to attain true spirituality if he lives under the existing and natural conditions of life, by discharging and respecting all obligations, both to God and his fellow-men. Therefore, those who renounce the world acknowledge their own weakness, and prove that they are not competent enough to fight down temptation. Such people are often acclaimed religious or spiritual by the ignorant masses, but the system is wrong. God does not wish it, and no true religion of His demands from human beings the renunciation of the world, or the non-participation in what has been especially created for them.

People adopt such views wrongly, and therefore the Qur-án was revealed to repudiate them and show the correct perspective. It is not wrong to say that Islam changed the entire religious outlook, by making it possible for human beings to attain spirituality together with participation in such things of the world. Concerning celibacy and the priesthood of the Nasara (or Christian) it is said in the Qur-án: "As for monkery, they invented it. We did not prescribe it to them, only to seek Allah's pleasure, but they did not observe it with observance." The Prophet says: "Islam does not recognize monkery." In the Qur-án there is much written concerning food, clothing and the like: "Who has prohibited the embellishment of Allah, which He has brought forth for His servants, and the good provisions." Which means that these are the benefits of true believers in this life, and that it is obligatory for them to participate in them. Once the Prophet advised a rich Muslim to wear handsome clothes saying "God wished that human beings show gratitude to Him by using the things He has given them."

On the subject of marriage there are clear and simple rules in the Qur-án, and the words of the Holy Prophet are: "To marry is to follow my example, one who avoids it is not of me." In all things the Prophet showed that spirituality does not mean just fasting and prayer, nor the renunciation of the world; he defined it as the height attained by prayer and fasting, along with the discharge of worldly obligations. In this wise the Prophet said that to maintain a wife according to the decrees of religion is also a good thing, and a means to the attainment of spirituality. A group of companions once wanted to renounce the world to that end, but the Holy Prophet forbade it, telling them to follow his own example, which was to fulfil one's duty to Allah as well as to the world. The Qur-án says: "If you love Allah, then follows me, Allah will love you." Millions have succeeded in gaining spirituality by following the example and teachings of the Holy Prophet, millions are succeeding and millions more will succeed in this only way.

The Qur-án was revealed to the Holy Prophet as the final and complete Book of God for the benefit of humanity. The world was a lost world, a sea of sin. Men had discarded all theories of the good and the spiritual. In the words of the Qur-án: "On land and sea moral degradation had settled." When the evil become universal, it was necessary to adopt a universal cure. The Qur-án says: "to-day your religion is made complete and perfect," which means that the religion that was inaugurated by God in the beginning of the world became complete on His sending the Qur-án through the Holy Prophet Muhammad. As a child is taught his alphabet, so God taught the religion of the world gradually, and little by little, by sending at different times, and to different peoples, His Prophets to teach His religion. When the world had reached that stage of understanding when it was ready for the final lesson, He sent the last and complete Book through Muhammad, for the perfection of Mankind, so that by following it men may attain to the goal of perfection.

It is right that the teacher of a religion so perfect should himself be a perfect man, so God selected Muhammad to be the guide and reformer of the whole world. God's words concerning the Qur-án are: "It is for all, seen and unseen," and concerning the Prophet, "He is sent by Allah as the Prophet for all." Because of this God granted him the title of *Khatam-un-Nabiyyeen,* which title not only means "the last of the Prophets," but also many things that go to prove that he was the greatest Prophet of Allah, and the benefactor of the world. One meaning of the word *Khatam* is ring, so the whole phrase means that the Holy Prophet encompasses all Prophets as the ring encompasses the finger. And it was because of this that he was made Prophet of the whole world; and the Book given to him was made to comprise the teaching of all the Prophets. God Himself says: "All the teachings of all other Prophets were this secured." The Qur-án comprises all other revealed books, and the Holy Prophet all the other Prophets. The word *Khatam* again means an ornament, therefore the phrase may also mean that the Holy Prophet is the ornament of all Prophets. All blame put upon other Prophets disappears under this phrase. So this clearing of the characters of the other Prophets was only achieved by the Prophet of Islam. Other books deny the presence of Prophets among people other than themselves, but the Qur-án says: "Allah sent Prophets to different people at different times, for the uplifting of their souls and for their guidance; therefore the believers should believe in all." It also connects all Prophets in a bond of love in these words: "All Prophets are brothers."

When the Holy Prophets attained Prophethood, and before his preaching, he at first met with abuse and was hooted and reviled. He addressed the people thus: "I spent the greater part of my life among you before becoming a Prophet, you all know that I never did wrong; but to-day you find fault with my teaching." They tried by all the means in their power to put an end to his preachings. He was tortured, abused, and put to many kinds of hardships, but never did he swerve from his duty to God. When the people saw that all they did was of no avail, they sought to tempt him by offering riches, women and position; but the Holy Prophet turned down their offer with the remark that he would not desist from his duty even if they brought the Sun to him and placed it on one hand and the Moon on the other. Throughout he remained steadfast in spite of all threats and all temptations. Any other man would have fallen in the face of such temptations, but he did not pay the slightest heed to the offers made to him; instead, by his example and teachings he showed a disgust for all the frivolous things of this life. He told his wives that if they hankered after the world and its luxuries, he would give them as much as they wanted, but they would have to go away. Nevertheless, he was so much respected and loved by them all that they said that they would rather stay with him and live a poor and simple life, than leave him and live a luxurious one. His examples of godliness and kindness were such that his most severe critics could find nothing to say against him. A man can at a pinch hide his true character before the world at large, but this he cannot do in his own home, and in his own home the demeanour of the Holy Prophet was so perfect that he was adored by all the members of his household. After his death his wives always remembered him, and shed tears at the loss of such an ideal husband.

I have already mentioned that God gave to the Holy Prophet the title of *Khatam-un-Nabiyyeen*, and I would add that the word *Khatam*, besides meaning a ring, ornament, etc., also means *Seal*; so that we can say that he was sent as the *Seal* of the Prophets, and that God meant his Prophethood to be the last, and that He will not send any more Prophets after Muhammad.

The Holy Prophet was a perfect example of poverty in riches. Later, when success brought plenty to Medina, he never partook of it. His was the heart that had only one image in it, and one purpose, that of Allah; there was no room there for worldly things. He would often say: "A simple house to live in, clothes enough to cover one, and some bread to eat, are quite enough for the sustenance of human life."

I have spoken before of the great miracles that the Holy Prophets accomplished for womanhood, and that before Islam woman was considered to be among the meanest creation of God. The followers of Jesus had called her a devil and the tool of the devil, because of the crucifixion of Jesus to atone for the sin of Adam committed at the instigation of a woman. Hinduism too gives her to better place than that of a slave and a servant of man. Krishna, who is often painted in the company of *Gopis* (milkmaids), when he attained spirituality, discarded them as beings unclean, but in the 6th Century A.D. the benefactor of the world changed the whole outlook on woman. From lowly and mean she became a being to be loved and respected. The Holy Prophet would often say: "Paradise is beneath your mother's feet."

In spite of his nearness to Allah, in spite of being the greatest of all Prophets, Muhammad used to say his prayers with as much zeal as though he was a lost soul seeking God. He would spend nights standing in prayers, regardless of physical pain; but what was mere physical pain to one whose heart was filled with Allah? He was never perfectly at rest unless he was in communion with Allah. He would pray for all. All peoples, men and women, young and old, were equally the recipients of his benefits, his kindness and his love. Even his bitterest foe found in him a friend. At a battle of Uhud the Holy Prophet was wounded, and knew that the enemy was bent on taking his life; but still he prayed: "Allah forgive them for they know not what they are doing." The people of Taif did all in their power to torture and harm him, and in return he prayed for them: "O Allah forgive them, give them the privilege of joining Islam and send them as friends to Medina." The Arabs were the greatest of unbelievers, but the kindness and love of the Holy Prophet succeeded in winning them over to Islam. And soon they were proud to submit themselves to the wonderful personality of the Holy Prophet.

The love and respect which a person wins in the heart of another depends largely on the benefit which that other derives from him. The heart of man is so fashioned that he is bound to love and respect those that do him good or some kind service. As there are infallible laws of nature, so there are of humanity, and any deviation from them, such as blind love or blind hatred, does not last long. A being who by his example does good and uplifts the soul of others is bound to be loved and respected. The proof of the following Qur-ánic saying is to be found in the histories of all nations: "For those, persons who believe in God, who believe in God, who always do good deeds, God gives love in the hearts of human beings."

Reason and careful study will lead one and all to admit the very great obligation which the world owes to the Holy Prophet. I do not say this because of my faith, but because of facts, and I do not think any one in the world, whether Hindu or Christian, will deny it. The real benefactors of the world are those who dedicate their lives to the good of humanity. Such people are found in all nations, and universal love and respect should be their portion. The doers of good, be they Moses, Rama, Krishna, Zoroaster, Buddha or Jesus, are, every one of them, to be respected. On the roll of benefactors the name of Muhammad shines out as the greatest; what he did for Arabia and the world at large, in so short a time, no other Prophet before him was able to do. Within the short space of twenty years the Arabs, who were the most ignorant, illiterate and superstitious of nations, became the greatest, the most learned and the most civilized nation of the world; he caused the disunited, scattered and least known nation of the world to established empires and devise laws of government that spread all over the world.

The Holy Prophet consolidated the Arabs; from a divided people they soon became a united nation, each and every individual working together and sympathizing with each other instead of fighting as before. Allah in the Qur-án says: "Thank God, Who had bestowed so many things for your benefit, before you were the enemies of one another, and fought among yourselves, but now Allah has made you regard one another as brothers by placing love and sympathy in your hearts."[1]

He made the life and the working condition of the slave tolerable by enforcing the same treatment for him as for a member of the family. The Islamic Brotherhood, which the teachings of the Prophet brought into being, did away with all social inequalities between man and man, woman and woman. He taught them to treat slaves with kindness and love, and made the liberation of a slave a meritorious act. He insisted that no free person should forcibly be made a slave, and that those who were already slaves should be treated as members of the family and granted freedom gradually. The Holy Prophet made it an obligation on the part of the Islamic Government to budget annually for the allocation of a certain percentage of the revenues to the purpose of the liberation of the slaves, by paying the ransom from the Government exchequer.

The Holy Prophet changed all misconceptions about women. He taught the Arabs to regard them as friends and companions, and to be kind and loving to them. He said: "A person who does not show kindness should not expect kindness from God." He taught them to regard infanticide as abominable and most displeasing to God, and thus it soon came to an end.

He had great regard for the rights of women; since the passing away of the matriarchal form of society women were, for the first time, emancipated by the Prophet. He showed, by his example, love, care, and respect that was due to them. And so woman, once deemed the lowest of the low, was raised up to a position of great dignity.

Is it any wonder, then, that the Christian historians of Europe should admit that of all the reformers and Prophets of the world The Holy Prophet Muhammad was the most successful and the greatest? His intention was great, and not restricted to one people or country as were those of the other Prophets. Any nation, be it Afghan, Turk or another, who sought for guidance, was helped and prospered. The brotherhood which he established comprised all races, black or white, weak or strong, great or small—all were made equal participants in the goods of the world. If the white had a right to become great and famous, so had the black and the salves; history records cases where slaves become kings. No one before Muhammad had conceived of such a brotherhood as this of the whole world; Muhammad, the greatest of God's Prophets, not only conceived it, but established it, and thus removed all barriers of caste, colour and race. It is, therefore, the duty of the whole world not only to recognize, but also to love and respect such a great and wonderful personality.

Muhammad came at a time when the world had extinguished all light given by the other Prophets, and was plunged in utter darkness and ignorance. Judaism, Hinduism, Zoroastrianism, and all the rest of the religions, had become religions only in name, for their followers had completely forgotten every principle. The last religion of the world before

Islam was Christianity; its principle were really true and great, but they were never put into practice. The depth to which the Christians had at this time fallen can best be explained by a Christian, Muir writes: "The condition of the Christians was most degrading,... and if Muhammad had not come... then the world would have always remained dark and ignorant." The words that the Qur-án used in this connection 1300 years ago are almost the same as those used by a scholar of to-day writing in the light of modern historical research. The Qur-ánic words are—"Corruption appeared in land and sea." And Mr. Dennison, discussing Islam in his book *Emotions as the Basis of Civilization,* mentions the following facts: "In the 5th and 6th century A.D. the world was standing on the verge of darkness. Ancient thoughts, the basis of which are emotions, and which made the existence of the world possible by teaching love and respect, were dead. There was no new light to take its place. It looked as if the civilization that was built in 4000 years was on the point of destruction, and that the world was about to go back to the age of complete darkness and barbarism...civilization, like a big tree the branches of which had spread all over, looked as if it were going to give way from the very root by being eaten up.... Was there anything that could have saved civilization and the whole world from destruction by uniting and consolidating all the forces?" Answering his own question, the author in describing the Arabs speaks of Muhammad, the Prophet of Islam, in these terms: "These were the people among whom was born a man who united the world from the East to the West in the Unity of God, and saved the world from destruction." Is it not correct, then, to say that Muhammad kept civilization alive in the world? Colossal is the obligation under which humanity lies to him, and greatly do I pity those who, instead of love and respect for the one and only benefactor of the world, have for him nothing but abuse, malice and slander. Such men should remember that the laws of God are infallible, and thus all will one day realize and acknowledge their obligation to Muhammad the Holy Prophet.

Success can only be achieved in the world by following the Holy Prophet. Fallen nations can rise only by taking heed to his teachings; the oppressed and the down-trodden can find happiness and peace only by obeying his instructions; the cruel can give up cruelty only by following the example of the Holy Prophet.

One of the chief troubles with the world to-day is that one nation is too fond of asserting its greatness and superiority over the other. Just because it happens to be a particular land where the people are white, it regards itself as superior, and looks down on those who are dark, deeming coloured people to be inferior in intelligence, manners and standards of life. The havoc and misery that this racial and colour prejudice has caused and is still causing can be better understood by studying the conditions of the countries where this question is an urgent one. Take, for instance, the "coloured" people of Africa and America. They will tell a tale that will shock the feelings of many. They will tell of the cruel treatment meted out to them by those "white masters" of theirs, and how wealth and position cannot help them in any way. There was a "coloured" man—an editor of a great newspaper in America. He married a white woman, but when he went to London on business, no hotel would give him accommodation. Why? Simply because he belonged to a "coloured" race. He had wealth, money enough to stay at the best hotel, but that was not the point. Once, a West Indian, an assistant Station Master, was travelling on board a steamer. He was never seen to take his baths, and when questioned on the subject, he said that he took baths daily, but he had to do it late at night. He dared not do so in the day-time. When pressed for the reason, he further explained that a few weeks previously one of his countrymen was on a voyage, he was seen using the baths and was very roughly treated by white men on board, because he said he had the audacity to use the same baths as the white men. A friend of mine tells me that a short time ago he was staying in India at a certain big hotel, and that among the numerous people there was an Englishman who had a dog. The Englishman was on speaking terms with my friend, and although well aware that the latter was an Indian, he often would show his dislike and contempt, and air his poor opinion of India and the Indians. Once he said in the hearing of my friend, "Indians bark! This dog of mine has more intelligence than an Indian!" That man, who called himself a "gentleman," was in all probability one of the many common and uneducated persons who come to India, to make their pile because of their white skins. That man, when he has made enough, will go back to his country, to live a fat and lazy life, with a nice big banking account and a cheque book ready at his hand, at the cost of the poor Indians he so much despised.

When you read the history of Islam, you will realize what is meant when it is said that the Holy Prophet removed all distinctions of colour and race between men and men, and brought them under one brotherhood of Islam. The coloured Muslims have no fear of being snubbed by the white men who embraced Islam. The Islamic principles have secured them the right of absolute equality, and encouraged them to activities in all directions of human effort and co-operation. There is in Islam no such thing as "inferiority complex" for they are taught that all human beings are equal.

One of the greatest benefits derived from the teachings of the Holy Prophets is in connection with education and learning. His words are: "Avoid ignorance, seek learning and always endeavour to add to it, and pray God to help you." The success of the European nations lies in the fact that they sought and still do seek education, learning and knowledge; those nations that are behind in learning are also behind in advancement and achievement. Without learning no advancement in any line is possible. The Muslims of to-day somehow seem to have lost their appetite for learning; they would rather waste in rubbish than read literature; they would improve their minds; and the result can be seen in their position to-day. Statistics show that there are no more than 7 per cent of them literate to-day. The world has known no greater educational reformer than was the Holy Prophet of Islam; and the fact that the Muslims of to-day are not as literate as they should be does not mean that the teachings of the Holy Prophet are at fault. The state into which they have drifted is of their own devising, and if they had only followed the example of the Holy Prophet they would have been far differently placed.

Reference

1. The Holy Qur-án. 3:102.

[***By:*** *—Al-Haj Qassim Ali Jairazbhoy*

Source: *The Islamic Review, Vol. XXII Nos. 11–12, Nov–Dec 1934.*]

2

MUHAMMAD THE MAN

Lives of great men all remind us,
We can make our lives sublime;
And departing leave behind us,
Foot-prints on the sands of time.

Since the dawn of human life, this planet has been visited by many a Prophet, Saint and Reformer; men of high calibre and outstanding personality; in and among different ages, places and peoples. As it has been admitted that until and unless we, human souls, take to ourselves a model by whose, example we may regulate life and conduct, it is impossible for us to "make our lives sublime," or to accomplish anything which deserves to endure. We require for that model a man of peculiar qualities—one who brings to us something new, refreshing and original. Who comes to us at first hand, a man of unflinching zeal, tireless, fortitude and peerless personality in emulation of whom should lie for us the way to that salvation which is the longed for bourne of the human soul.

Let us, therefore, survey the mysterious expanse of the History of the World, and find out for ourselves which of its innumerable suns and stars shine upon and illuminate it the most, and on whose shoulders the mantle of the Ideal for mankind at large is best fitted to repose.

Let us take the writers first, Ghazzali, Rumi, Sa'di, Firdausi, Ibn-u'l-Muqaffa, Hafiz and Tabari, Homer, Shakespeare, Dante, Voltaire, Milton and Euripides, showed to the world the rightful superiority of language over feelings, as well as that of imagination over language. They have shown us how language is able to vivify the object of its praise, to leave a permanent impress on the minds of its readers; to cleanse, like pure water, the soul and, through the soul, the body, and to take, as it were, a distinct photograph of the processes of human thought.

Cicero and Byron, the great champions of liberty and patriotism, the masters of feelings and passions are for us familiar figures; we recognize the patriotism and the noble fortitude of Socrates and Demosthenes, who, fired with the Divine Spirit, waged a tireless crusade for Truth, Righteousness and Emancipation of their fellows from the strangle hold of evil conventions and meaningless rituals which prevailed among the Greeks up to the very last moment of their precious lives. Rousseau and Oliver Cromwell, the Lord protector of England, are of those who, perceiving the evil canker of vice draining the life-blood of their peoples, came with their respective remedies and succeeded in cutting down the evil and curbing the most carnal desires of their peoples, thereby revealing to them the path of Peace whereby alone they might attain to the Kingdom of Heaven.

Luther and Calvin, those noted reformers, imbued with a mighty zeal for combating the evils of the Church of Rome, protested against the wrong teaching of the Pope, and the world came to know of the false and corrupt teaching of Christianity—Christianity which had originally been free from any sort of mischievous alloy. They were firm and adamant in their resolve to expose the hypocrisies of the priests and the ignorance and the slave mentality of those to whom they preached, caring no whit for the numberless troubles and obstacles encountered on the part of both clergy and laity.

Washington, Garibaldi and Alfred the Great are among the few peerless personalities of world-fame who fought for the welfare, prosperity, settled government and freedom of their respective countries. Again, the Carthaginian Hannibal, and Julius Caesar the Roman, both of them masters of magnanimity and courage before whom the heights of the highest mountains and the depths of the deepest oceans dwarf into insignificance were men, who, utterly sincere in their devotion each to his motherland, died like happy warriors fighting for the noble cause of its freedom; while the scientific and philosophical achievements of Bacon, Newton, and Epicurus gave a new and profound insight into the mysteries of the Universe, representing thereby to us at the same time the greatness of its Master. For this we owe gratitude to them, as also to Plato, Solon, Galen, Pythegoras, Euclid and Aristotle, the master minds of old Greece, for teaching us the immutable principles of learning.

I also recognize the large heartedness, the greatness of soul, the force of reason and the wisdom, the sublime law-giver Solon in whose code reposed the secret of the wonderful and rapid progress of his country; of the great romantic Charles Dickens, whose very Novels were potent in removing the barbarous laws and customs then surviving in his country; of Addison and Johnson, who inspired in their fellow-countrymen the zeal for literature; of the revered Mathre, who, for the first time laid the foundation of the census—that wonderful system whereby the king may see at a glance the doings and details of and concerning his kingdom and his subjects; of Adam Smith who raised the standard as well of humanity as of civilization by introducing the Science called Economics, another important branch of Learning; of the great reformer Seneca who advocated justice as the essence of Law, and wrote volumes on Metaphysics and Theology; of the mystical King Arthur of the Round Table fame, himself the mirror of justice and the benefactor of the poor and the down-trodden; of great Ulysses, the King of ancient Ithaca whose wisdom and whose wanderings have been themes for poet through all the ages, from Homer to Tennyson. Of Polyenus, the noted writer on War, that most important science of destruction both peace and mind, of Huntrede who made known to the world of the Art of Agriculture by his exquisite poetic compositions; of the great Historian Latoshe whose History of Rome inspired one hundred and forty heroes; and of all the masterminds both of East and West for their learning, wisdom and nobleness of heart. But among them all have not found one by following in whose footsteps I can reach my goal. I have not found my Ideal.

Again, when I consider Adam, the father of humanity, Noah and Abraham, David and Solomon, Joseph and Jacob, Ishmael and Isaac, Moses and Jesus, my eyes do not linger on them—though it must not be assumed from this that I do not believe in the verse: "Do not differentiate between one Prophet and another." On the contrary I believe, as do all Muslims, that all the prophets who were sent to ameliorate the lot of humanity were prophets of Islam, which means peace and perfection—and I feel discouraged and sad at heart. But when I conjure up for myself the lovely, loving and lovable personality of the Prophet Muhammad (on him be peace!), that paragon of beauty, that quintessence of creation, that Leader of and Intercessor for humanity, that finest blend of all that is best in man, I am refreshed and take courage. If Adam was the "deputy of God," Noah "the saved one," Abraham "the intimate friend," Ishmael, "the sacrificed one," Joseph, "the beautiful one," Moses, "the mouthpiece," and Jesus "the spirit of God," Muhammad was all in all. In him we find merged all the qualities of his fore-runners. He is the perfect personality as described in the couplet: —

> Husn-e-Yusuf, Dam-e'Isa Yad-e-Baiza dâri,
> 'Anchih Khubân hama dârand, to tanhâ dari.

which being translated, runs: "Thou combinest within thee all that was individually given to Joseph, Jesus and Moses, to wit, thou hast the beauty of Joseph, the reviving breath of Jesus, and the white hand of Moses." In other words, in Muhammad was concentrated all that was individually possessed by Joseph, Jesus and Moses, all in fact that we would see in a perfect man.

In spite of all the great characters it has produced the world, with all its groups, colours, habits and conventions is yet in dire need of a single and unique personality who, notwithstanding all differences of religion, culture, caste, colour, complexion and language should yet be common to all, and acceptable to all. Such a personality, as described above, is found in Muhammad, the Hero of Islam, which is the Universal Religion, a true Prophet, and a true Man who, realizing the social and the religious vices gnawing at the heart and poisoning the life-blood of the human race came with a remedy—a remedy perfect and permanent in its effect. God, the most High calls him " The Mercy for the Worlds," for the Qur-án declares most emphatically: "And We have not sent thee except as the Mercy for the Worlds."

Again, the mission of each and every prophet and personality as mentioned above, was limited to the cultivation of a particular trait of human character. Thus, the life of each of the above persons represented a model in this or that branch of human morals, but the life of the Champion of Islam embraced human nature in its entirety, and raised it to the acme of perfection. In his own life, every phase of human morals found complete manifestation, and he is, on this very account, called the PERFECT EXAMPLE for humanity.

In the Mosaic dispensation, prophet after prophet made his appearance to serve as a model in one particular line, but the illuminating star of Arabia, by himself, combined in his own person and in a much higher degree the collective virtues of all the Israelitish prophets. The manliness of Moses, the tender-heartedness of Aaron, the generalship of Joshua, the patience of David, the grandeur of Solomon, the simplicity of John, and the humility of Jesus, all merged in him. Thus every patriarch sent forth but one ray—a single beam of light, in one particular direction, but the Star of Arabia, whom God calls " The Mercy for the Worlds" (not of a particular nation or community) was sent to give light to the whole Universe. He knew no jugglery or deceit: he was neither poet nor magician, as the Western world has called him. He was the

Apostle of Allah, the Most High—the centre whence radiated everywhere Light for World.

The greatness of a man consists not at all in the working of miracles, nor in preaching or in the formulating of theories; these are but transient activities. His greatness is to be found in a mighty and comprehending personality, an attribute responsible, like prayer, for working wonders indescribable. "Personality," says the Sage of Working," conciliates opposition and inspires love, respect and imitation, which result, in the long run, in implicit obedience. It changes ideas and revolutionizes thoughts." I would rather say that it creates a new basis for the better actions of generation after generation of the human race. Muhammad (peace be on him, and on his descendant), is such a personality, and therefore unique. "If the test of a great man's inspiration is the reverence which his personality radiates and his words inspire in the hearts of those who acknowledge his divine origin," says an Englishman, "then Muhammad must be numbered amongst the greatest." The test *is* right, and Muhammad *is* a unique figure and character, in view of the devoted love and implicit obedience that he inspired in his followers, who were not persons of inferior standing or mental calibre, but men of rank, wealth, culture and position, as well as in his own kith and kin, who knew the intimate facts of his life.

It would need volumes to describe the versatility of character of the Prophet, and at the same time, I am confident that History will never be able to show any personality other than the Prophet Muhammad wherein we may find the assemblage of all the virtues, human and divine; the virtues that constitute and evolve humanity, which is a problem of very complex nature; I mean humanity in its various aspects—physical, emotional, sentimental, social, moral, mental and spiritual. To do justice to this super-man, to his sincerity, generosity, frugality, broadmindedness, firmness and tenacity of purpose, his steadfastness, his calmness in adversity, his meekness in prosperity, his humility in greatness, his modesty of character, his anxious care for animals, his passionate love for children, his bravery and fortitude, his magnanimity of spirit, his unbending sense of justice, and, above all, his noble mission, volumes, indeed would be required. These and many more are the phases that can be depicted and portrayed by the pen. Let me, therefore, before I turn to the later days of his life, describe, in the words of the late and greatly lamented Rt. Hon. Sayyid Amir Ali (may his soul rest in peace) the Prophet's life that he lived in Mecca, the place of his birth and of his Call:—

"We have seen this wonderful man as an orphan child who had never a father's love (we all know that the prophet was a posthumous son of Abdullah, son of Abdul Mutlab) bereft in infancy of a mother's love and care; his early life is so full of pathos; growing up from a thoughtful child to a more thoughtful youth. His youth as pure as his childhood, as austere as his boyhood, his manhood as pure, sublime and devout as his youth. His ears ever open to the sorrows and the sufferings of the poor and the weak; his heart ever full of sympathy and tenderness towards all the creatures of God. He walks so humbly and so purely that men turn round and point. 'There goes Al-Amin, the true, the upright, the trustworthy.' A faithful friend, a devoted husband, a thinker intent on the mysteries of life and death, and on the responsibilities of human actions (the aim and end of human existence) he sets himself to the task of reclaiming and reforming a nation, nay, a world, with only one loving heart to comfort and to solace him. Baffled, he never falters, beaten, he never despairs. He struggles on with indomitable spirit to achieve the work assigned to him. His purity and nobleness of character, his intense and earnest belief in God's mercy bring round him many a devoted heart, and when the moments of the severest trials come, like the faithful mariner, he remains steadfast at his post until all his followers are safe, and then betakes himself to the hospitable shore, such we have seen him, we shall see him now, the king of men, the ruler of human hearts, chief, lawgiver, and supreme magistrate, and yet without self-exaltation, lowly and humble.

Henceforth, the preacher, who with his own hands mended his clothes and often went without bread, was mightier than the mightiest sovereigns of the earth."

Before the contact of Western culture with Islam, the enemies from the various opposite camps poured forth torrents of abuse on the Prophet, but "Muhammad is no longer an imposter, but a great reformer. He is no longer a neurotic patient suffering from epilepsy, but a man of tremendous character and unbending will. He is no longer a self-seeking despot, ministering to his own selfish ends, but a beneficent ruler shedding light and love around him. He is no longer an opportunist, but a prophet with a fixed purpose, and a man of strong will, undeviating in his consistency." All this Europe has acknowledged and acknowledged freely too. Thomas Carlyle and Gibbon, gifted writers, both have, each in his own way, done full justice to this man, in whom merges all that is best in humanity and whose personality combines within itself all that is required in a man. His whole body was permeated with the Divine Love, so to say. In fact, he was so much in love with his Maker that his whole life was devoted to an up-hill struggle for Truth, the ultimate goal of all wordly striving. Davenport and Bosworth Smith in English, Krehl and Gremence in German, and Caetani in Italian have opened to the Western world vistas of the life of the Prophet which demolish completely the stock arguments employed by Christianity against this benefactor of the human race. George Bernard Shaw, whom somebody has called "the Voice of To-morrow,—addressing us To-day," has studied both the man and his creed, which is not merely a system of Theology, but a perfect civilization in itself, and feels not the least hesitation in accepting him as True Man in the real sense of the word. Inspired by his simple, sincere and sweet creed. Shaw has, in one of his most recent books, emphatically declared that within a very short time, this world will have only one religion, Islam; for he believes that that man is in all essentials a Muslim who believes in the Unity of God, the Equality of Mankind and the Prophethood of Muhammad. In his "Saint Joan" he brushes away all the wrong notions and biased views of the Christians against the Prophet of Islam, whom God Himself describes as "The Mercy for the Worlds" (*Rahmat-ul-lil 'alamin*).

While the achievements of every great man are, as I have said before, limited to a definite sphere, those of Muhammad (peace be on him) cover the entire field of human conditions. If, for example, greatness discovers itself in the reclamation of a degraded nation, who can have a better claim than he who lifted up a nation sunk so low as were the Arabs, and made of them the torch-bearers of Culture and Civilization? If greatness lies in unifying the discordant elements of a society into a harmonious whole, who can have a better title to the distinction than he who gathered together a people like the Arabs, split up into warring tribes severed by generations of blood-feuds. If greatness consists in establishing the Kingdom of God on Earth, there, too, he stands unrivalled. If greatness lies in displaying high morals, who can be a match for one who was referred to by all foes included, as "Al-Amin," the Trustworthy? If conquest determines the greatness of a man, surely, even here, history cannot find the like of the Hero of Islam, the Champion of Humanity who rose, as we have seen, from a helpless orphan to become a mighty conqueror and a King, nay, an Emperor of an infinite Empire of Islam which has withstood storm and stress all these thirteen hundred and fifty-three years. If the *living driving force* that a leader commands be the criterion of greatness, has name, even to-day casts of charm as of magic over four hundred millions of souls spread all over the habitable world, binding them together at the same time irrespective of caste, clime, colour and creed, with the strong yet pliant cord of Brotherhood.

Muhammad (peace be on him), was peace-loving, and a peace-maker by nature. It was mainly on this account that he preferred the Peace concluded at Hudaibiyya to continued bloodshed, though, according to the terms of that Peace or rather Truce, the concessions obtained were almost nil, and the Muslims were treated as though conquered. Notwithstanding the fact that warfare was alien to his nature, he was, by sheer force of circumstances, driven to take up arms and lead his soldiers to battle. For war, like polygamy, is a necessary evil, and there are certain times when it becomes inevitable. How could he be a perfect example to humanity at large had he refused to resort to arms? He is, as we have seen, a perfect model, and as such, had to pass through many difficult times.

In word and action he was the same. He was the best of men, nay, the only man, who himself put into practice all the principles he taught to others. He was the exact antithesis of that one sung by Shakespeare, who

> ..... like a puffed and reckless libertine
> Himself the primrose path of dalliance treads,
> And recks not his own rede.

There is not a single ordinance or injunction from above that did nit find complete manifestation in his own action. "We read homilies and sermons elsewhere, we find idealistic and unpractical theories of morality and ethics," says the Sage of Working, "but we fail to find them in their own teachers." Muhammad is the only and noble exception, who practised rather than preached. In other words, his morals were the Qur-ánic verses. How can the precepts and homilies that are not practised by their own-teachers infuse into others any enthusiasm or any electric waves of acceptance? Surely, we are not to be guided by those who "reck not *their* own rede." The actions of teachers for more than their words should entitle them to our allegiance. "In fact, an ethical aphorism written on a wall is as good as in the mouth of a teacher, if he has never been able to put it into practice," says that brave soldier of Islam, Khwaja Kamal-ud-Din. The History of Christianity would have been quite different had there been some actions of its Law-giver to explain his precepts. With due difference to all the religions of the world, and to the disparagement of none, I declare most emphatically that none can dare to prove the contrary of the fact that whatever the Prophet preached, that he practised. We have no concern whatever with what the teacher has in his mind. "Potentiality is no proof of actuality." Mere lip-teaching does not at all show us what we have to do. Saying is quite another art than doing. It furnishes no proof that we possess the morals which we preach to others. Action is the thing. In that way, every one of us is a hero, if only we be given a chance. But what of man who neglects the time and opportunity afforded him? Words and ideas converted into actions can alone show our worth.

It was no fault of Jesus that he could not translate all his sayings into actions for he had not such opportunity or occasion for moulding the various moralities into practical shapes as had Muhammad. Almost all the moralists seem to have laboured under two disadvantages. Firstly, they did not pass through the vicissitudes of life as did Muhammad, and secondly, though they did their best, they could not complete the task before them. On the other hand, those who had such chances, and who took full advantage of them, have left us a very meagre record of their lives, and that record, not the true narrative of the actual events. Muhammad's, then, is the unique personality of which both the records and the experiences satisfy all that could be demanded of a true prophet and a real man. In fact, his whole life was an eloquent and practical commentary on the Holy Qur-án.

Muhammad as a ruler also entered into treaties with his enemies. Who would at times demand his assent to terms that were derogatory both to his mission and his personal honour; yet even then he would accept them and act on them and observe them under all circumstances, whereas the Western Political Conscience feels not the least compunction in breaking covenants and throwing promises to the winds. In the battle of Badr, the numerical strength of his followers was much inferior to that of the enemy. During the retreat two of his followers lagged behind, and were cut off and made prisoners but released on the understanding that they would on no account rejoin the Prophet. They, however, returned but when they told their story he lost no time in sending them back to those with whom they had made their covenant, though at that time the Prophet could not afford to lose a man. Again, after the truce with the *elite* of Mecca, he would not allow any of his followers to join him at Medina.

Though himself illiterate, the Prophet enjoined the acquisition of knowledge upon all Muslims, both male and female. How would say to his followers: "Acquire knowledge from the cradle to the grave." "Acquire it even if you must go to China to find it." "To seek after knowledge is incumbent on both man and woman." "Teach your children as best as you can." He would often remind them of the words of God Who says: "Whosoever is given knowledge, is given in reality much goodness." At times he would exhort the assemble to acquire knowledge of anything and everything that the world contains. He was often heard to say: "The Pen is mightier than the Sword, and a drop of ink from the writer's quill is more sacred than the blood trickling from the wounds of the martyr." For he knew full well the value of knowledge which "gives a man a clear conscious view of his opinions and judgments, a truth in developing them, an eloquence in expressing them, and a force in urging them. It teaches him to see things as they are, to go right to the point, to disentangle a skein of thought, to detect what is sophistical, and to discard what is irrelevant. It prepares him to fill any post with credit, and to master any subject with facility. It prepares him for the world." Knowledge is an inexhaustible treasure, the more you draw from it, the richer it grows. An ignorant person is, in fact, so much lumber, which is seldom wanted in life, if not a curse on society.

In the administration of justice Muhammad was scrupulously even-handed. Muslim or non-Muslim, friend or foe, high or low, young or old, all were alike to him. Even before he had received the *Call*, his impartiality and integrity were admitted on all hands. People would bring their disputes to him to be settled. Even the Jews, the most inveterate enemies, both of his mission and person, would recognize his honesty and abide by his decisions. Just, in the highest sense, even in the treatment of his servants, everywhere he observed the same principle of equality. Anas, his slave, is reported to have said that during the ten years he was in the service of the Apostle of Allah, he was not once reprimanded by him. Whenever the *elite* of Mecca were unable to solve a problem or remove a difficulty they used to bring the case to him, and he, out of sheer good-will, would settle the question in such a way as to excite among those present admiration for his power of judgment, and wonder at the mental balance which always retained so stable and equipoise.

Self-sacrifice, too, was one of the most prominent characteristics of the life of the Prophet. He had four daughters, of whom *Bibi* Fatima, the mother of Imam Hassan and Imam Hussain, was the youngest. It fell to her to perform, by herself, all the household duties. Once she asked her father to get her a servant to help her but he refused flatly saying that she could herself do all she needed. Being the head of the State, there would have been no difficulty in procuring a servant or servants for her, but he did not wish that she should make herself dependent upon others. Whenever presents were made to him, though he disliked intensely the practice of giving and accepting such things, he distributed them there and then amongst his friends. Once a woman gave him a piece of cloth, which he, being in need of it, accepted. One standing by began to admire it looking upon it with envious eyes, whereupon the Prophet gave that piece of cloth to him straightaway. Gardens, they say, are rarities in Arabia and the most coveted of landed properties. Once a person presented the Prophet with somewhere about seven gardens. These he accepted and devoted them to charitable uses, their produce being distributed among the poor and needy.

Firmness in his dealings, disregard of social distinctions, modesty, lenience, shyness, humility, hospitality and sublimity of disposition are among the chief traits in the character of the Prophet. Some one has remarked that "the humble soul is like the violet which grows low, hangs its head and hides itself within the folds of its own leaves. Were it not that the fragrance of its many graces discovered it to the world, it would choose to live and die in secrecy." In Muhammad, indeed, were all these characteristics of the violet, and, yet like musk, his fame spread all over the world. Humility and meekness dwelt in his bosom from the very beginning, and for ever. Meek to the highest degree, he enjoyed a perpetual Sabbath. His anger was like fire struck from steel, hard to be roused, and when roused, soon gone, for meekness not only imparts great peace of mind, but adds lustre to the countenance and the thoughts behind it.

Man is a social animal. He must live in society. He will, nine cases out of ten, never be happy without society. Beset as we are with numerous impulses and cravings, our inability to satisfy them by our own unaided efforts demands the formation of a very strong and well-organised force for the purpose. This force is called *Society*. Islam is the most democratic of all religions. Whereas every other religion without exception admits a number of grades and caste-systems, Islam ignores them all. Democracy, the most-worshipped goddess of modern times, was first conceived of by the Prophet of Islam. He it was who advocated Universal Brotherhood. Snobbishness in all its grades is to be found everywhere, in every department of human activity. Even the sacred institution of religion is not immune from its baneful influence. Hinduism, though one of the oldest in the world, yet limited in extent and scope, to a greater degree than Islam and Christianity, has welcomed the veritable monster of snobbishness in its most refined and polished shape. In fact, Manu, its Law-giver, has raised this social canker to the dignity of a virtue. Untouchability is the bane of human society. This dragon of Untouchability was from the beginning a curse, and has remained so ever since. But, as "the old order changeth yielding place to new," and as the Law of change is the law of God, Mr. Gandhi, the sole monopolist of Yervada Gaol, has been sent to uproot this mandrake of a plant—Untouchability, which leads to social and communal disruption and destruction. He has launched the crusade against the centuries-old conventions of Hinduism, and I pray that he may succeed in his noble mission in raising the social status of the *Harijans*, the souls of God, but unfortunately, the object in view is more political than social or religious, and for this reason alone, if not for others, Mr. Gandhi is bound to fail.

As for Islam, it does not permit any such thing. It is like a pure honey which requires no chemical purification. It is immune from all such diseases as aristocracy, snobbishness, aloofness, and despotism. It is the only religion that not only teaches and preaches Universal Brotherhood and Equality, but puts them into actual practice. It binds all its adherents with the common cord of God, Love and Brotherhood. By it we are taught to look to one another's needs, to make sacrifices in favour of those who are around us, to cultivate a spirit of Universal brotherhood and to discipline self-seeking tendencies which, if not properly controlled and regulated, will work havoc on humanity and create every sort of trouble. Islam is not only easy to follow, but is the most liberal religion in the world. Seeptre and Crown in it are as good as at scythe and spade. Bolshevism, the greatest post-war movement of the world, is Islamic in its spirit, the only difference being its negation of God. Muhammad can rightly claim to have discovered the specific remedy for controlling the self-seeking tendencies in man, for the remedy he suggested and acted upon is none other than that Universal Brotherhood whereby he purged Arabia of all its troubles.

It was Muhammad who took up the cause of Woman, Woman who had been treated as a chattel in the pre-Islamic Era. No religion or civilization had, till then, done anything to raise the status, up to which she was born. In dealing with women, Muhammad is poles apart from the rest of the Prophets and other spiritual luminaries throughout the ages. The Hebrew Law was unfavourable to her. A Jew, invoking the blessings of God prays: "I think Thee, O Lord! And Glory be to Thee that Thou didst not make me a woman." She was no better off in Judaic society. She had been called "the organ of evil," "likened to a scorpion ever ready to sting," "the poisonous asp," "the malice of the dragon," and described by many others with like outrageous epithets. Such was the esteem in which Woman was held by persons of exalted position in the Christian Church, like St. Paul, St. Bernard, St.

Anthony and others. St. Paul seems to be the originator of this attitude. His personal grudge against the fair sex is, perhaps, the consequences of his suit having been rejected by a young Jewish woman, the daughter of the High Priest. Even Jesus could not bring himself to ameliorate her lot. At the time when the early Christian Fathers were raising the slogan *woman was made for man and not man for woman*, Muhammad told the world *that woman was the twin half of man*. The Holy Qur-án calls her "Muhsinah," the benefactor, which means that she merited none of the curses heaped upon her by the Christians and the Hebrews. Muhammad showed the world that she "was a rocky fortress against Satan, a light-house of virtues, a garment of man as he is her garments and a fountain of love and affection." Woman is a ministering angel for man, and it is thus that Islam thinks of her.

Muhammad (peace be on him) was also averse to slavery. He thought of its abolition thirteen and a-half centuries ago. The modern world did away with it only comparatively recently, whereas the Prophet had practically abolished it in his own lifetime. He would purchase slaves only to set them free.

Let me conclude with the rich and wonderful words of the late Khwaja Kamal-ud-Din who, in one of his books, says: "In him we find a child, a young man, an elderly man, a son, a brother, a husband, a father, a neighbour, a persecuted fugitive, a soldier, a general, a conqueror, a play-mate, a statesman, a king, a judge, a law-giver, a man in adversity and a man in prosperity. Varied as are these various positions, you will find him the same man from beginning to end, a thorough gentleman, to use the English phrase, always unchangeable and unchanged in his temperament. In his dealings, in his general mode of life."

Such was Muhammad, may Allah shower His choicest blessing upon him and his family!

[***By:*** *—Sayyid Arif Shah, B.A.*

Source: *The Islamic Review*]

3

THE CHIEF OF THE PROPHETS

Muhammad was born in the city of Mecca, on the 12th of Rabi I, corresponding to the 29th of August of the 570th year of the Christian era. The prophet was of high birth, being of the family of Beni Hashem, the Princes of their country, the noblest of the Qureish tribe of Arabia, which for several descents together has been the chief ruling tribe of the country. His grandfather was the custodian of the Kaaba. Such was the family in which the Holy Prophet of Islam was born.

He was fatherless from birth, he lost his mother when only six and his grandfather when he was hardly nine. Notwithstanding his high birth and noble parentage he was thus left poor, an orphan boy. He was adopted and brought up with utmost care and tenderness by his uncle Abu Talib who took him to Syria on a commercial expedition of a thousand miles by camel caravan at an age when a child is expected to be sent to school for acquiring knowledge, receiving training. But he was doomed to stumble down in deserts. Camel-tracks in the sand were his only alphabet, and the tales of raiding and briganding of merchants and mights of Arab tribes, told round the caravan fires at night, his only history and adventure book.

While on a halt at Busara, he met Buhaira, an Arab monk of Christian faith, who, fixing his scrutinizing gaze upon the young traveller, was so wonder-struck by the signs of future grandeur and splendour of his intellectual and moral qualities that he at once recognised in the orphan boy the future saviour of mankind. Accordingly the monk impressed his convictions of Abu Talib saying: "Return with your young charge, protect him from Jewish treachery and guard him from the machinations of his enemies; for great dignity awaits your nephew and truly he is born to achieve great things."

Just at the both of Muhammad, his mother's brother, who himself was an astrologer, predicted that Muhammad would rise to a vast power, build a mighty empire and establish a new faith among men.

The predictions of his maternal uncle, the convictions of the Christian monk, the prophecy of Jesus Christ and the Prayer of Abraham were fully justified in the event of Muhammad's becoming the chosen Messenger of God, to redeem humanity from sins and ignorance, unite the discordant heart of Arabia as the heart of one man and teach to the world that "There is no Deity but Allah."

Under the tender care of his uncle Muhammad grew up a handsome boy, and his most amiable qualities and sweet and gentle disposition won him the affection of all who happened to come in contact with him. But from his early youth he was quiet and reserved, thoughtful and or reflective mind and given to pensive meditation. When his companions wished him to join them in their amusements, he would say: "Man is created for a nobler purpose than indulgence in frivolous pursuits."

In the prime of manhood he was handsome and of proper stature, square-built and sinewy, joints well-knit together, with hands and feet large, shoulders broad, and the chest open and wide. He had a firm and healthy constitution, and was uncommonly strong and vigorous. He was of spare figure, carrying presence with it, of majestic aspect, comely presence and an engaging address on the whole. His head was massive and well-shaped, his forehead noble and high, broad at the temples and across it, down to the eyebrow ran a prominent vein, a feature of the Hashemites, which used to swell and throb when he was angry or excited. He had a frank oval face, marked and expressive features, brown noble, arched and joined; a Napoleonic nose, finely chiselled and attenuated at the end. His eyes were large, black and piercing, full of the lustre of the light of prophecy, and his peculiar magnetic power, and fringed with eyelashes dark and long. His cheeks were thin and ruddy with robust health, and mouth large and flexible, indicative of eloquence with graceful smile; and the teeth pearl-white and regular. His neck was long and well-moulded which rose like a pillar from his ample chest; his hair was jet-black, soft and curly and fell down to his shoulders; and his voice sweet and sonorous. He had a beard long and full, and moustache that added dignity to his appearance. His complexion was very fair and ruddy, and his skin clear and soft. He was in his steps quick and firm like that of one descending a hill, and when he walked he made use of a staff after the manner of the prophets.

Now as to his moral and intellectual perfection, and natural gifts and virtues. He was a man of attractive personal attainments with beautiful qualities; he had an acute and sagacious wit, powerful retentive memory, quick apprehension, vivid imagination, a calm and equable deportment, majestic mien and bearing, a patriotic spirit and steadfast perseverance, a genius to command and expect obedience from equals as well as inferiors; he had an undaunted courage, serious, sincere character, capable of real amiability, a very acceptable address, elevation of mind, delicacy and refinement of feeling. He was simple, kind and tolerant in his domestic life, attractive in his manner, sympathetic with those in trouble, kind and considerate to his friends and family, and a tender father and a generous husband. He was a man of excellent judgment, sweet and pleasant in conversation, inoffensive in behaviour towards his friends, and of great condescension towards his inferiors; he was very courteous both in giving and receiving visits and he was a very great lover of children; he would stop them in the streets, pat them on their little heads, speak a few kind words to them; he expressed disgust at a man who having ten children declared that he had never kissed one of them, and he hated nothing more than lying. He was in fact a solid, dependable, brotherly, genuine man, affectionate and magnanimous and austere in his religious practices, brave and zealous with a clear conception of the work that lay before him, and he was above reproach in his personal and family conduct. Usually he was grave and dignified, taciturn and reserve, yet he indulged in pleasantry and in congenial company he did unbend and enter into the social pleasure of his family, friends and disciples alike. He was sober and abstemious in his diet, and with no magnificence in the matter of dress which was always of cotton and sometimes of wool, often coarse and patched. He abhorred strong drinks. He was very scrupulous about personal cleanliness and ablutions. He had the genius alike to influence the learned and equals and command the illiterate and inferiors, and soothe the great men with praise and relieve the poor with gift. His applaudable commanding presence, his ready eloquence, and charming aspects always engaged on his side the attention of public and private audience alike, and he gained many over to his side, as much by the charm of his manners as by the doctrines he preached, and we find that he was able to control self-willed and masterful persons like Khalid and Omar.

His unconquerable will, unshakeable resolve, fixedness of purpose, thorough-going perseverance, unyielding persistency, indomitable spirit, interminable patience, calm endurance, irresistible courage, and the stamp of the nobility of character that he bore, mark the special features of the life of that Great Arabian Prophet.

His admirable politeness to the great, his applaudable affability to the humble, his dignified demeanour to the presumptuous, his universal benevolence and courtesy, his equable treatment of friends and strangers, the powerful and the weak; his respectful attention to the rich, his generosity to the poor, naturally endeared him to those who came in contact with him, and procured him respect, admiration and applause.

His uprightness of character, and correctness of demeanour and his honest dealings with the people won him the love of friend and foe alike, and exalted him over the rest of his countrymen so that by common consent he was called *Al-Amin*—The Faithful, The Trusty, long before he became the chosen Messenger of God the Almighty. In short, from the standpoint of physical and moral purity, natural gifts and qualities, Muhammad was in every sense the essence.

Muhammad began his prophetic career when he was 40 years of age.... In order to realize the stupendousness of his work it is necessary to have a knowledge of the condition of Arabia of his times. He came at a time of much mental agitation in Arabia. The Arabs and the Jews outvied each other in superstition, idolatry and moral depravity. The greater part of Christendom was steeped in abject credulity. Belief in the illogical supposition that 3 is 1 was considered to be the sole means of salvation. The Church of Christ was rent by factions, and false teachings prevailed. The world had in fact entered the Church. Muhammad lived at a time when Christianity was a flower that had been plucked to adorn the temple of idolatry. Not only were the nations sunk in idol-worship, but Christianity itself had become so contaminated with paganism that a mere lip acknowledgment of God was confounded by the false declaration that God was a trinity of persons, in plain words, that there were three gods: a doctrine which is as idolatrous as belief any of the pagan deities. Not only had the Kaaba within it 360 idols affording the worshippers a separate god with every new sun, but each tribe had a battalion of other images and fetishes which served the purpose of a family or personal deity, and in addition to these people approached reverentially every white and beautiful stone they chanced to come across. They worshipped the sun, the moon, the stars, fire and water and heaps of sand where stone could not be found. In short they worshipped anything that appealed to their imagination and sought a god behind every natural event. To the independent haughty Arab, there could be no law, for they yielded to no rule, no government, no justice; for they acknowledged no supreme authority, and roved through boundless desert and enjoyed unfettered freedom. And there could be no progress, for there was no plan acceptable to these Arabs, full of cunning and subtle knavery, the untamable race of all the world, wild haters of towns, dwellers of wilderness, who despised and scorned the very comforts of a civilised life. This was the state of affairs in Arabia—the blasphemy against God, the degenerate Christianity of his time and the polytheism of the Arabs—among which he lived. The unmitigated evil of the fetish worship, social evils such as the burying alive of girls, and promiscuous sex relations, the tribal blood-feuds and wars, the rough and dangerous life of fervour and fighting, looting and briganding, and consequent national weakness of his own people aroused the gentle soul of Muhammad and set him abrooding gloomily over these evils prevalent at the time.

Now in considering distinctly and briefly as to how Muhammad shaped the destiny of his people by civilizing the Arabs in as many tens of years as Christianity required thousands to civilize its Teutons; and how the seeds were sown almost of every development political, intellectual, moral and spiritual; and how the religion was established in the unprecedented period of twenty years, without the aid of any royal patronage and support; how without parallel in the history of humanity the rapid victorious spread of Islam was effected; why Islam met with so unexampled a reception in the world; why multitudes of converts swelled the ranks of the faith—one has but to refer to the simplicity of the creed which has been ever a part of its charm—the pure, rigid, austere monotheism—a belief in the One absolute God, which alone renders Islam feasible—free from priestcraft or elaborate doctrinal trappings; the noble doctrine of the duty of man to man, of man to lower creatures; and the universal peace, kindly feeling and good-will towards each other that it teaches; the profound conviction of the Unity of God that it creates in men; the fraternity, the republic of equality of all men, irrespective of colour, race, nationality and class; the equal support and consolation and peace of mind that it so unreservedly gives to all who believe and confess; and the sobriety, general good and admirable morals which it inculcates; the genuine conviction kindled by the spectacle of its victorious strength; its moral and spiritual stability; its chastening and ennobling ideas; its calling into activity many of the noblest forces in the nature of men; and on the whole patriarchal piety and moral rectitude of the believers which are the strongest recommendation to the seekers after truth and are among the most obvious forces at work in the religious and missionary activities of Islam whose system, as a whole, is capable of lending itself to a very vital force of religious life and has a commanding appeal to its immense range of followers, the appeal of loyalty to a man, to a message, and to a brotherhood.

The last and the mighty proclamation of the Great Arabian Prophet, the very essence and personification of centralization and concord, was that "an Arab has no superiority over a non-Arab, nor has a non-Arab any superiority over an Arab. You all are the children of man, and man sprang from the dust. Every Muslim is a brother unto another Muslim; all Muslims are brethren."

It is a tribute to this message of human equality and of human fraternity that Islam has no sects diametrically opposed to each other like other religious, say, Christianity, which has now well over four hundred sects. The sole nursery of lofty thoughts and noble actions lie in the conception of the equality of man before God, and it was Islam that at last conceived it first. All creatures that are made by him are brothers bound together by indivisible kinship. Islamic fraternity has an international spirit and if ever the impossible becomes actual it does become by its marvellous touch. Islam gave in the ultimate form the most perfect description of brotherhood, the equality of all men, pulling down one and all barriers of rank and of race, of birth and of breeding.

No student of religions with profundity of knowledge and convictions would find the same spirit of equality in other religions. We see the present day facts that among the Hindus a rigid caste system is rampant everywhere. They believe that the people of certain caste are born from the head of the Creator, others from the hands and feet and some from limbs which it would be indecorous and indecent to mention here. In Judaism and Christianity, which claim sisterhood with Islam, we find that the former rejoices in considering the Israelites only to be the chosen people of God while in the latter a particular terminology "native Christians" is coined by the Christian priests to distinguish them from their more lucky brothers who were born in Europe.

Colour or race, make no difference to it. Islam, in fact, is above all such petty differences. She draws no hard and fast rules, has no such violent antipathies, bigotries and prejudices as Christendom or other religious systems. Colour in her eyes is no disgrace, no bar to God, much less, therefore, to human fellowship and assimilation.

* * * *

Muhammad is an historical character. We know him as a neighbour, a father and a son. We know him as a husband, a businessman, and a friend—no truer friend than Muhammad over lived—who was never first to withdraw his hand from the grasp of another who offered him his. We know him as a teacher, a reformer, and a master whom it was alike impossible to disobey and impossible not to love and who wept like a child on the death of his faithful servant. We know him as a gentleman, a warrior, and a general. We know him as a noble, a saint and a prince, but above all petty differences and superior to titles and ceremonies. We know him as a camel driver, as the *Al-Amin,* and as the Prophet, but he never claimed the power of working miracles; we know him as a legislator, a Caesar and a Pope but he was Pope without Pope's pretentions and Caesar without the legion of Caesar, without a standing aımy, without a body guard, without a palace, without a fixed revenue. If ever a man had the right to say that he ruled by a right divine, it was Muhammad; for he had all the power without its instrument and without its support. Further, we know him as a man of uncommon genius, poor by his own choice so that when lord over the whole of Arabia he did not even build a brickhouse for himself. Personal ambition and aggrandizement never entered his mind, lordly airs he never assumed, nor personal services he ever demanded. From the beginning to the end with the simplicity natural to a great mind he loved to perform the humblest of the offices of his daily life. Just imagine, the Lord of Arabia tended the flock, milked the goats, swept the hearth, kindled the fire, patched the garment, and even mended his sandals. Dates and barley bread were his usual fare, and milk and honey all his luxuries. His frugal hut and the leathern mat to sleep upon were all his household appointments and the luxury and splendour of an Oriental despot; we know him as a poet, but illiterate himself, scarcely able to read or write, he was yet the author of a Book which is a poem, a code of laws, a book of common prayer, and a Bible on one, and is reverenced to this day by a sixth of the whole human race as a miracle of style, of wisdom, and of truth. It is one miracle claimed by Muhammad—his standing miracle he called it, and a miracle indeed it is.

The Holy Qur-án, on the one hand, is most unsparing in its condemnation of debauchery, hatred, calumny and slander, pride, envy, vainglory, falsehood, revengefulness, mockery, hypocrisy, avarice, uncharitable judgment, prodigality, mistrust, and suspicion, bloodshedding, usury, slavery, persecution, polygamy, thirsting after worldly good, and excesses of every description, while on the other hand, it is emphatic in insisting on the virtues of benevolence, almsgiving, liberality, patience, charity without any distinction of caste and creed, temperance, modesty, courage, faith, humility, frugality, straightforwardness, endurance, submission, toleration, mildness, justice, especially towards orphans and widows without respect of persons, filial piety, obedience to divine commandments, gratitude towards God, fidelity to engagements, ransoming of captives, forgiveness of injuries, love of place and truth, decency in speech, returning good for evil, showing kindness to strangers, and above all the Holy Qur-án enjoins in most emphatic terms that Muslims "should implicitly obey and yield to the ruler or government of the time in observing strictly the laws promulgated." In view of this Qur-ánic injunction a Muslim taking part in thwarting the government of his time and disobeying the laws of his ruler not only infringes the laws of his government, but also makes a clear departure from his religious obligations, and disobeys the commands of his Holy Prophet, and thereby rankshimself among the infidels.

It is due to these merits that from the Atlantic to the Ganges the Holy Qur-án of Islam is acknowledged as a potpourri of pure, elevated and benignant precepts, just and benevolent sentiments, lofty feelings of humanity, fundamental code of theology, legal statutes—civil and criminal jurisprudence—military organisation, a deep moral earnestness, sententious oracular wisdom and elements on which mighty nations and conquering empires can be built up, and the Qur-án is a friend of the poor on the whole.

Furthermore, the Holy Qur-án admittedly occupies the most important position among all the religious books of the world; it deserves the highest praise for its conception of the Divine Nature; it is the most widely read of all sacred scriptures on the face of our Globe; it is the only Book that teaches a rigid and austere and purer and stricter Monotheism than the Books of all the Religious Systems of the Universe and as such "this book will go on exercising a most potent influence." Its influence one day would invariably succeed in controlling the lives of all human races as one. It will stand as a stupendous monument of solitary legislation and proclaim the miracle of style and poetic genius of its Author.

I make bold to say that a careful reader of the Qur-án and an inquiring mind cannot come to conclusion other than accept the true and reasonable tenets of the Holy Book of Islam as the most suitable to our time and age; a man who should observe them would lead a virtuous life. And this is, I presume, the highest ideal of human existence. Islam is more suited to our world than any other faith. Islam has elements in itself that would most adequately satisfy and administer to the exigencies of our time and age. I venture to say that if the world in its wisdom feels the necessity of a religion, Islam is the only rational and peaceful faith that a sane man can accept, and boast of being one of its fortunate votaries.

We read that every Prophet had a standing virtue, a characteristic of himself to distinguish himself from the masses. But Muhammad in his quality of Prophet united in himself the meekness of Abraham, the sincerity of Moses, the trustworthiness of Ishmael, the patience of Jacob, the humility of Solomon, and the abstinence of Jesus which differentiated him not only from his compatriots, but likewise eminently exalted him above all the famous prophets of the Old Testament or the other prophets the history of humanity has ever known.

Thus Muhammad is manifold founder of a nation, of a religion, of an empire, and of a republic of Islamic fraternity. He established for the first time in history a united Arabia, founded an empire with self-supporting elements and strength in itself; he established a religion—Islam—with a book, the Qur-án, the Muslim Gospel, which is the glorious testimony to the Unity of God, and whose creed is free from ambiguity or suspicion.

Muhammad stands unparalleled on the pinnacle of renown as a man, as a hero, as a saint, as the most successful of all the prophets and religious personalities, as the chosen and the seal and the last of all the prophets.

If only one of the many reforms, for example, the Islamic Brotherhood, inaugurated by the Holy Prophet of Islam were to be taken into consideration, his being the true benefactor of mankind must be admitted by all; and the Great Arabian Prophet must be loved and honoured by all for his valiant championship of *"making brutes men and men divine."*

MUHAMMAD'S APOSTLESHIP

Before discussing the validity of Muhammad's claim to Divine mission, we must solve the question, "What constitutes the real criterion of Apostleship?" Broadly speaking, two criteria of prophethood have been prevalent the world:—

(1) Performance of miracles by a claimant, *i.e.,* he displays super-human actions, we are led to believe that he is divinely gifted and hence he is a messenger of God.

(2) Reasonableness and purity of a claimant's teachings and actions, *i.e.,* if we by an impartial examination of his worlds and deeds come to the conclusion that he stands for a right cause and guides humanity or a section of it to a right course in all spheres of life, then we pronounce our judgment in favour of his claim.

Needless to say that the second criterion takes a more rational view of the case than the first. The first which is liable to a variety of objections (such as, counterclaims by magicians and sorcerers, etc.) will hardly be accepted by the modern world. The second may, therefore, be taken as a safe criterion of prophethood.

Muslim doctors and divines are also divided on the question of the criterion, some favouring the first and others the second. Razi says:—

> Believers in prophethood are divided into two groups. One holds that miracles prove a man's claim to apostleship, whereas the other maintains that we should first set up a criterion of truth both with regard to belief and observances and then we should see whether the man in question seeks to guide the people to the right path, and also whether he is capable of influencing them in the choice of right. If he satisfies the above condition, we are led to believe that he is a true prophet.[1]

Ibn-i-Khaldun in his well-known *Muqaddama* (Prolegomena) divides mankind into three classes:—

(1) Perfect beings who are divinely gifted and have successfully realized the aims of life and reached the Destination.

(2) Middle-class people who are travelling along the road leading to the Destination.

(3) Worthless men who are at a standstill or have gone into degeneration.

Naturally, Divine messengers belong to the first class of mankind. They having reached the Destination take up the noble task of leading the masses to the right path and guarding them against evil.

After keeping in view the true criterion of prophethood as discussed above, the question "Does Muhammad satisfy the conditions of prophethood?" becomes easy of solution; provided, of course, we study his life and teachings in an impartial and unprejudiced manner and without any personal and racial considerations.

A comparison of the Pre-Islamic condition of Arabia in all its aspects with the condition obtaining there at the time of Muhammad's death will undoubtedly convince even the most stubborn critic of the genuineness of Muhammad's claim to the Divine mission. Can there be any shadow of doubt about the prophethood of one who, himself unschooled and unlettered, reformed the character of one of the most licentious peoples on the face of the earth, who purged Arabia of all its evils and vices, who grouped together the warring camps of the Arabs into one great commonwealth, who established one Universal Brotherhood with One God to worship, one Code of Law to follow, who purified the mode of living introducing decency and nicety in every walk of life, who clearly defined the standard of morality, who equalised rights and privileges for men and women, and last but not the least who regulated human life in all its spheres in the most rational and practical way?

I may refer here only to one aspect of the life-career of the Prophet of Islam, *viz.,* sense of equality and absence of self-exaltation. Muhammad was born as a poor orphan and died as an undisputed master of Arabia. Between these two extremes he had to pass through various stages of life, but history testifies that at every stage he was one and the same. We do not find a grain of difference between Muhammad the Orphan and Muhammad the recognised leader of the land. Humility, purity and sanctity characterized every turn of his life.

An obedient son, a devoted husband, an affectionate father, a faithful companion, a sincere friend, a successful leader, a thorough gentleman and above all a practical man, he inspired respect and admiration even in the minds of his bitterest enemies. The late Khwaja Kamal-ud-Din of Woking fame rightly observes in his masterpieces, entitled *The Ideal Prophet:*

> Muhammad is the best exemplar, and, I may say, the only Prophet who himself worked out all principles he taught to others. Whatever he taught to others, he practised himself.

One of the chief causes of the rapid success of Islam was the absence of distinction between the Prophet and his followers. Muhammad was both a leader and a follower, a commander and a soldier. Never did he issue any order which he himself did not carry out. It is natural that we are tempted to follow a leader who is one of our own rather than one who is above us and beyond our reach. Jesus poorly failed in his mission, simply because he appeared or was represented as super-man, and the people found it impossible to follow in his footsteps. We can adore a super-man, we may even worship him; but we cannot possibly follow him. Muhammad repeatedly warned the Believers against paying him more respect than was due to him. God says in the Qur-án:—

> Say (O Muhammad) verily I am a man like unto you (and) it is revealed to me that your Lord is One.

This is why we find that Muhammad issued repeated warning against the practice of "prophet-worship." In one of the Traditions he is reported to have said:

> Do not respect me in the way in which the Christians respected the son of Mary. Verily, I am Allah's slave; and speak of me as the slave of God and His Prophet.

This unequalled amiability and humility of the founder of Islam was not confined to the fold of the Believers only. Non-Muslims were also entitled to the same generous considerations of the Prophet. Hardpressed by tortures and persecutions at the hands of the infidels, the Believers requested the Prophet to invite the Divine wrath upon the persecutors; but he replied magnanimously saying: "I have come here as a blessing to humanity, not as a curse."

An European Muslim, formerly a Christian, in the course of an article entitled "Islam, My Only Choice" published in the *Islamic Review*, says:—

> My surprise knew no bounds when I began to read to Muhammad. Like a panorama the events of his life passed before my eyes one after the other. From the cradle to the grave everything of note in his life is narrated and preserved in a well-authenticated record. I was amazed to find in him an assemblage of the best of characteristics so rare in others. I am at a loss to understand how he could unite in himself all the best qualities of discrepant characters. He is meek and at the same time courageous; modest as a maiden but the bravest of the soldiers on a battlefield. While with children loved for his playfulness and endearing talk to the little ones; when in the company of sages and old men, respected for his wisdom and farsightedness. Truthful, honest, trustworthy, a reliable friend, loving father and husband, a dutiful son, and a helpful brother, Muhammad is the same man whether in adversity or prosperity. In short, judge Muhammad from whatever angle of human character you will, and he is nowhere wanting.

The late Syed Amir Ali while describing the events of Prophet Muhammad's life at Mecca says in his *Spirit of Islam* :— "We have seen this wonderful man (Muhammad) as an orphan child who had never known a father's love, bereft in infancy of a mother's care, his early life so full of pathos, growing up from a thoughtful childhood to a still more thoughtful youth. His youth as pure and true as his boyhood; his manhood as austere and devout as his youth. His ear ever open to the sorrows and sufferings of the weak and poor; his heart ever full of sympathy and tenderness towards all God's creatures. He walks so humbly and so purely, that men turn round and point 'there goes *Al-Amin,* the true, the upright, the trusty.' A faithful friend, a devoted husband; a thinker intent on the mysteries of life and death, on the responsibilities of human actions, the end and aim of human existence,—he sets himself to the task of reclaiming and reforming a nation—nay, a world, with only one loving heart to comfort and solace him. Baffled, he never falters; beaten, he never despairs. He struggles on with indomitable spirit to achieve the work assigned to him."

[***By:*** *—Syed M.H. Zaidi,*
Source: *The Islamic Review, Vol. XXII, Nos. 11–12, Nov–Dec 1934.*]

4

THE MERCIFUL MUHAMMAD

And not alike are the good and the evil. Repel (evil) with what is best, when lo! He between whom and you was enmity would be as if he were a warm friend. And none are made to receive it but those who are patient, and none are made to receive it but those who have a mighty fortune. And if an interference of the devil should cause you mischief, seek refuge in Allah, surely He is Hearing, the Knowing[1].

And the recompense of evil is punishment like it, but whoever forgives and amends, he shall have his reward from Allah, surely He does not love the unjust. And whoever defends himself after his being oppressed, these it is against whom there is no way (to blame). The way (to blame) is only against those who oppress men and revolt in the earth unjustly, these shall have a painful chastisement. And whoever is patient and forgiving, that most surely is of the affairs the doing of which should be determined upon[2].

Muhammad stands out prominent in having successfully established the unity of Allah. It implies two most difficult operations: eradicating idolatry of long standing which had become part and parcel of the nature of the Arabs, and imparting instruction in the Oneness of God. The stronger the hold of a false doctrine on the hearts of a nation, the more vigorous and patient endeavours does it call for on the part of a reformer. The Apostle of Allah displayed a marvellously sympathetic and resolute heart in undertaking the correction of a nation which was passionately given to idolatry and superstition. His grim determination and untiring zeal for the extermination of the worship of fetishes called forth an equally violent and terrible opposition. Every tribe adored its own idol, and manifested vehement indignation in standing up for the vindication of its traditions. The whole of Arabia made common cause and rose in war against Islam, which stood for consummate obedience to Divine laws ingrained in human nature and codified in the Qur-án. The terribly hot opposition assumed the form of active persecutions, especially when the Arabian Prophet had been pursued into Medina. He had to experience, indeed, a very rough time of it. The Qur-án sketches the doleful picture which necessitated struggle on the defensive: —

"Why should ye not fight in the path of Allah, and for the weak among men, women, and children who say, 'O, our Lord, bring us forth from this city whose inhabitants are oppressors; give us a champion from Thy presence, a defender!' "

Invaded on all sides by the belligerents, he was constrained to take the field occasionally or to send out his men to meet aggressors. The chequered career of reverses and successes provided an excellent opportunity for manifesting the various phases of the character of the Prophet. No trying circumstances, no ordeal, no violent opposition could keep him from working in the direction of the unity of Allah. When successful no recollection of atrocities inflicted on him and his companions was ever too strong for preventing him from meting out kindness and forgiveness to the vanquished foe. It is by dint of his noble character and genuine sympathy that he cherished for mankind, and mercy that he showed to the enemy, that people crowded to Islam. Compulsion engenders hypocrisy, and has nothing in common with sincerity. The followers of Muhammad have always signalised themselves for their devotion to Muhammad and Islam. This speaks for the charm that the doctrines possess, and refutes the baseless charge that Islam was spread at the point of the sword.

The following episode occurred in the seventh year of the Flight, when the concerted forces of the Jews and convulsions. The treacherous treatment that was designed to extinguish the life of their Divine leader, and that brought about the sudden and tragic death of one of the choicest flowers of Islam, made the camp indignant and furious beyond bounds. The scene can better be imagined than described. The enraged and victorious hosts demanded instant retaliation.

Ordinary commanders are carried away by the tide of strong feelings of their men. Nay, they seek pretexts for committing violence and pillaging the fallen folk. But Muhammad was pre-eminent in enjoying freedom from such diplomatic craft. He had already granted them quarter, and would be true to his word even at the cost of heavy price. He sent for the conspirators and required them to state the entire plot. They were reluctant in disclosing the story and attempted in vain to throw Muhammad off the track. At last the culprit admitted her guilt. Now think of the present war and wanton violence that has been incessantly practised on the slightest pretexts, and think of Muhammad, whose own life was threatened, who was victorious and in a position to inflict exemplary punishment on the miscreants, and who was pressed by his hosts to meet out exemplary punishment to the ungrateful foe. What should he do now? Could he not consult his convenience and his furious followers? Could he forgive without incurring the displeasure of his comrades, who were justified in vindicating vengeance for mean perfidy? Should he not avail himself of the opportunity that offered for compelling the people to embrace Islam? The Holy Prophet Muhammad was invincible to all such impulses. He was possessed of a remarkably strong but charitable character. He considered the question and forgave the offender. Even the hostile writers have had to record this memorable event, which is so eloquent of the idolatrous Arabs were defeated at Khaibar, and the town fell. Merciful and magnanimous as he was, Muhammad extended general forgiveness, and assured the disbelievers of the safety of their life and property. He sojourned there for three days, and before quitting the place for Medina he fell a prey to a conspiracy.

The mercy and kindness that the humiliated inhabitants of the fallen city met with at the hands of the Prophet was requited in a very cruel and cowardly manner. They conspired to kill him. They knew his virtues. He was very sociable, had no arrogance about him and readily reposed confidence even in the vanquished foe. They contrived to beseech him to accept a gift of roasted mutton. The Prophet would not disappoint them. They felt overjoyed, and readily set to work to give effect to their shameless scheme. A fanatic was selected for the discharge of the task. Zainab, who boasted descent from a well-known warlike family and whose uncle Marhab had suffered a very crushing defeat in the recent battle—Ali having cloven his skull with his heavy scimitar—was agreed upon as the right instrument. The exasperated lady, in whose bosom fanaticism was rivalling with thirst for wreaking vengeance, used her craft in charging the roasted mutton with the deadliest poison, concentrating it mostly in the shoulder, which she came to know the Prophet liked the best. The plot was almost successful, and the Apostle was near falling a helpless victim to it. The viand was placed before him and his adherents. The Prophet partook a small quantity and then spat it out instinctively as it were. But Basher, who had been demonstrating wonderful feats of strength and prowess in the field of battle fell prostrate on the spot. A warrior, who was adamant against sword and spear, fell an easy prey to the guiles of a vile wretch. His death struggle was unbearable; he expired in the midst of writhes various aspects of the noble heart of The Holy Prophet. Undoubtedly it argues an incredibly large patriarchal heart. To such irresistible and fascinating traits of the Apostle Islam owes its rapid spread and diffusion. The ignorant critic does not realise that this is a far sharper instrument than the sword to break the stiffness of disbelief.

Muhammad was not a man who would only theories and talk of "humanity" and "forgiveness". In his life one studies everything practised, and his precept invariably coupled with his personal example presents a personality which is gloriously ideal. The Qur-án is justified in depicting him as an exemplary character: —

"Verily a noble pattern had ye in Allah's Apostle, for all who hope in Allah and in the latter day and oft remember Allah." —The Holy Qur-án, 33 : 21.

References

1. The Holy Qur-án, 41: 34–36.
2. *Ibid*, 42: 40–43.

[***By:*** *Khwaja Salah-Ud-Din Ahmad*
Source: *The Islamic Review, Vol. XXII, Nos. 11–12, Nov–Dec 1934.*]

5

Glimpses from the Life of the Prophet Muhammad

"We (God) have not sent thee (Muhammad) otherwise than mercy unto the nations" (The Qur'án, 21:107).

"Blessed be He who sent down 'Al-furqán' *(illumination) on His servant, that to all nations he may be a warner"* (The Qur'án, 25:1).

HUMAN SOCIETY AT THE ADVENT OF THE PROPHET MUHAMMAD HAD SUNK TO ITS LOWEST EBB.

If the world ever needed a prophet it was at the time when Muhammad made his appearance, when the laws of God were being violated and the limits and bounds put by Him were being transgressed simultaneously on the whole surface of the earth. Every gross degradation of humanity has always seen the appearance of a prophet, so when the whole horizon of the world had become darkened under the dense clouds of infidelity, dishonesty and unchastity, the Great Prophet came in Arabia. It was a time when every country and each nation had seen complete depravity; so much so that sin was not regarded as sin in many cases, but as an act of virtue. The statement may startle many, but it is truth, and a reference to the Church history of the mediaeval days in Europe and of the Puranic age in India, as well as the Mazdaic history of Persia, will verify our remarks. Human society at that period of human history had sunk to its lowest ebb, spiritually as well as morally. And "as in Nature, light always follows darkness and rain comes after drought", so this wretched state of things then obtaining in the four corners of the world in the fifth century of the Christian era called either for the appearance of several prophets in several countries or the advent of one masterly mind who should come to restore universally the religion of God in its perfect form. Different nations before Muhammad had been given different books, but the books could not remain free from human alloy; the will of God revealed to man had become obscure, and diversity of opinion cropped up everywhere, even in most essential principles of religion. The Qur'án refers to this state of things in the following verse, where it refers to the necessity of the Qur'ánic revelation:—

> *"(All) people are a single nation, so God raised prophets as bearers of good news and as warners, and He revealed with them the book with truth, that it might judge between people in that in which they differed, and none but the very people who were given it differed about it after clear arguments had come to them revolting among themselves, so God has guided by His will those who believe the truth about which they differed, and God guides whom He pleases to the right path"* (2:213).

In commenting upon this verse, Muhammad 'Alí writes in his English Translation of the Qur'án:

"The first part of the verse states the universal law according to which Allah raised prophets among all nations, because all the nations are a single people, and therefore it could not be that prophets should be raised in one nation and not in another. With every one of these prophets, we are then told, a book was revealed, so that it might point out the right way to the various contending parties that existed before the advent of that prophet. But as time passed, the very people to whom the book was given so that they might follow it, went against it. Thus, though a prophet had been raised in every nation, yet every nation had forsaken the right way and acted against the very direction which had been given to it, so difference again arose which necessitated the advent of another prophet. Hence it was necessary to raise a prophet who should show the right way to all nations. If a prophet was needed by every nation to settle its own differences one was surely now needed to settle the differences of the various nations, for the truth which had been shown to different prophets had again become obscured. Thus among the different national religions of the world Islam occupies the position of an international religion."

The logic in the above is obvious. It seems to me quite clear and convincing. The Divine dispensation has always deemed it necessary to enlighten man of the high will of God, and of the index of His heart. And it was done before Islam came by such books as the Old and New Testaments, but all those books which were revealed before Muhammad became obscured and unauthenticated, so there was a genuine need of another revelation. Besides, the world was on the move to bring the distantly located units of the humanity into one cosmopolitan body, and therefore a book was needed to accumulate all the past truths purified from human alloy a prophet was needed to mirror the life of all other prophets. Hence the Qur'án came, and the Prophet Muhammad came —the Qur'án as the Final Testament or Gospel, Muhammad as the *Seal* and the Last of the Prophets.

THE REASON WHY MUHAMMAD IS THE LAST PROPHET

But why the last? A full reply to it demands a study, which present space at my disposal hardly allows: but I may take here one aspect of the question. Let us consider the primary object for which the mantle of prophethood falls on the shoulders of a chosen one. He does not came for any personal aggrandizement nor to become an object of worship and to take the place of the Deity. He brings a message from God to man for the guidance of the latter, from Heaven and translates them into action through his own example. He is the first to obey the laws revealed to him from Above and leads others to follow him in doing the same. Thus the words of God and the actions of a prophet in the way of illustration help others to pursue the path of guidance, and if they are preserved in their original integrity and transmitted to us in their genuine colours, there lies no necessity of having a new revelation or a new prophet. But the fact was that whatever had come from God before the advent of Muhammad saw corruption and human interpolation. The records of the lives of the pre-Islamic religious teachers themselves are enveloped in mystery. They are more of the character if a myth than of history. In fact, we know very little of their life. Hence the need of the Qur'án and the Prophet Muhammad. And if the Qur'án is just the same as it was in the days of the Prophet, and the record of the acts and sayings of the Prophet Muhammad himself is unexceptionally complete, faithful, and correct, are we still in need of any other prophet, or any new revelation from God? Hence the Qur'án, the last Book of God and Muhammad, the Last of the prophets. It is more on account of the finality of the Law and guidance given in the last message of God than the personality of the holy messenger which makes him the Ultimate Prophet. When the Holy Qur'án faithfully represents the will of the Most High and contains everything necessary to meet our moral and spiritual requirements, a new revelation would be a useless repetition and a redundancy.

MUHAMMAD "THE MOST SUCCESSFUL PROPHET"

That Muhammad was the only prophet who could see his mission fulfilled in his own life-time is a simple historical truth. The chief characteristic of the *Holy Book revealed to him which no other book can claim is the wonderful transformation which it brought about,* and it is to this characteristic also that it lays claim in the very commencement when it says: "This Book, there is no doubt in it, is a guide against evil." That the transformation wrought by it is unparalleled in this history of the world is admitted on all hands; for if the Prophet Muhammad was "the most successful of all prophets and religious personalities," this success was due to no other cause than the Qur'án. Its injunctions swept off the most deep-rooted evils like idolatry and drunkenness and left no trace of them in the Arabian peninsula, welded the warring elements of the Arabian society into one nation, and made an ignorant people the foremost torch-bearers of knowledge and of science. Besides, every word of the Qur'án gives expression to Divine majesty and glory in a manner which is not approached by any other sacred book; and hence the challenge of the Holy Qur'án remains unanswered to this day.

The whole human race, leave apart the Arabs, was at its lowest moral ebb when the Qur'án was revealed. Clouds of darkness and ignorance overhung the horizon of the earth. Libertinism was the order of the day; so much so that wickedness of the blackest dye was taken in some countries as an act of merit in the eyes of God. In four corners of the world all laws of God had been violated and Divine limits transgressed. And the Arabs were the most wicked people that the earth of God had ever seen. They not only committed wrongs of the worst type, but they exulted in doing so and were great boasters of it. That was an age of the best poetry in Arabia. They used to meet in their fairs and festivals and vie with each other in their power of making poetry; they produced and read the finest specimen of their composition, and it often contained narrations of their villainous deeds. A people of this sort! And within less than a quarter of a century transformed into a nation of God-fearing men of piety and righteousness, keeping all the commandments of God and respecting all the laws of society. The most ignorant of the world became torch-bearers of knowledge and learning to the then benighted world. Those who kept the weaker sex at the lowest stage of degradation became the first champions of female rights, and infused into the world such a chivalrous spirit as was unknown before. And this all within the shortest space of time! History fails to refer to another regeneration like what was effected by Muhammad.

SPIRITUALITY IS THE SECRET OF SUCCESS OF THE PROPHET MUHAMMAD

This success, so unique in its kind and so unparalleled in history, only speaks of that highest stage of spirituality which the Prophet Muhammad had attained. No reform in any community can possibly be worked out unless its members entertain some regard for the reformer and are willing to obey him. But no worldly riches or power, nor even any amount of one's working miracles, can inspire others with that love, respect, and obedience which always following advanced spirituality. The words of Muhammad were got the dictates of a potentate. Nay, he disavowed always possession of things which might influence others in his favour. In the words of the Qur'án, he would say often and often: "I say not to you, 'In my possession are the treasures of God'; neither do I say to you, 'Verify I am an angel'; only what is revealed to me do I follow." But still he commanded submission and homage unimaginable. In fact his words were the words of the beloved, to be respected and cared for by the lover. And if such is the mental attitude of the people towards their teacher, no wonder he is "the most successful among all other religious personalities" in working out reforms. But one should first reach the height of the ladder of spirituality before one aspires to that success. Jesus might convert water into wine, but he could not convert the nature of his disciples into what he desired them to be. He wished they could possess a grain of faith. And his apprehensions proved true when the trial came. One mostly trusted betrayed him. If others deserted him, the one given the keys of heaven cursed and disowned him. Call them what you will, "infirm in faith" or "weak in spirituality," but the fact remains the same. It does reflect on the weakness of the teacher's spiritual influence. He seems to lack that "alchemy' which converts a base metal into shinning gold. The followers of Moses also would not care much for their liberator. They would not listen to him on his way to the Promised Land. But the Companions of the Prophet Muhammad would always say: "Like the companions of Moses, we will not say: (O Moses) 'Go thou and thy Lord and fight.' but we will fight on your right and left, in your front and on your back." And these were not mere lip expressions. Invariably they were put to hardest trials, and their words proved always to be true. The following unparalleled piece of bravery and fidelity of the Prophet's companions read in various books like the *Sahíh* of Bukhari, the *Sírah* of Ibn Hishám, and *The Life of Mahomet* by Sir William Muir.

UNEXAMPLED DEVOTION OF THE COMPANIONS TO THE PROPHET MUHAMMAD

It was in the battle-field of Uhud, in one of his defensive wars, when the Prophet Muhammad, being hard pressed by the forces of the enemy, fell down in a pit and fainted.

He had received over eighty wounds: two of the rings of his helmet had run into his cheek, his face weltered in blood, and a blow at his teeth made one of them fly away. The enemy was marching on and sending volleys of arrows, and the lift of the Prophet was in danger. He being knocked senseless and no breastplate to defend him against the enemy, disappointment and despair were staring him in the face, but the self-devotion and fidelity to their master, the unprecedented characteristic of the followers of the Prophet, warded off the dire consequence of the situation. Abú Bakr, the first successor after the Prophet, was the first to see the danger, and was foremost in offering ready help, which example was at once followed by 'Alí, Talhah, Zubayr, Abú 'Ubaydah, Abú Dujánah, and many others. The Prophet was in the pit, and a sure mark for the enemy. The fight being hand to hand, and the place being even and plan, the only fortification which could save the leader at the moment was a living wall of the human beings, which, however, was not wanting. They fortified the pit and exposed themselves to the coming volleys. The human fortress gave a brave defiance. Talhah strained two or three bows, and received thirty-five wounds in the endeavour to shoot back the pressing enemy, and proclaimed that no blow would reach the sacred body of the Prophet, but through his own chest, and besought his esteemed leader to refrain from raising his head, and thus obviate the danger of any arrow striking at him. Abú Dujánah was afraid, lest the weak flesh in him should overcome his faithful love for his master; he, therefore, turned his back to the enemy and inclined over the Prophet. The other constituents of the living fortification made an impenetrable wall against the arrows of the enemy. They fell dead one after the other, but their vacant places were filled up by others equally devoted.

There were no hospital assistants or the sisters of charity to nurse the wounded, but love and devotion made up the deficiency. Abú 'Ubaydah applied his own teeth to extract the rings of helmet firmly embedded in the cheek of Muhammad, and hand to lose his own two teeth before he succeeded in his endeavour. Water could not be found at that moment to wash the body and face of the Prophet besmeared with blood, but many a human tongue came forward to lick it off. Fátimah, the daughter of the Prophet with Safiyyah and other renowned women, were busily engaged in staunching the flow of blood and nursing his wounds. But it was Umm Nusaybah, the daughter of Ka'b, whose courage greatly contributed to win the day. She wielded her sword and drew her bow with the object of defending the person of the Prophet that lay in the pit, other ladies like Umm Sulaym, Umm Salít, 'A'ishah, caught her enthusiasm, and accordingly made an onslaught on the enemy, while nursing the wounded.

One of the young children was commanded by his mother to arm himself with a sword and dash upon the enemy to defend the Prophet.

The above speaks volumes of the teacher and the taught. The followers of Muhammad proved true to their professions, which they used to sing proudly as their warcry:

"We are that very people that have pledged themselves to Muhammad to fight in defence of their faith with our"

MUHAMMAD AN IDEAL REPRESENTATIVE AND GUIDE OF HUMANITY

"A noble pattern have ye in God's Messenger" (The Qur'án, 33:21).

"For thou (Muhammad) art of a noble nature" (The Qur'án, 68:5).

"Say, 'If ye love God, then follow me (Muhammad)'" (The Qur'án, 3:29).

The spirit infused by the Prophet did not only find its exhibition in the use of arms, but it enabled "the sons of the desert" also to face courageously the most formidable of the foes that a man has to grapple with—his own corrupt nature and evil habits. History fails to refer to a single instance where a reformer met such an implicit allegiance to his precepts from the people he wished to reform, especially in the matter of eradicating their most deeply rooted evils. "Drink" was one of their evils. No Bacchanalian orgies elsewhere could surpass the Arab indulgence of alcohol in those days. Their daily meals were three, but they worshipped Bacchus five times a day. But when the time came for the Prophet to introduce into them total abstinence, the streets of Medina were overflowing with the detestable contents of the wine-barrels, which were emptied at the one magic word of the Prophet Muhammad. One word from the master-mind, and the five times fixed for the worship of Bacchus were converted into the five times of God's worship in Islam. Such radical revolutions in the morals of people cannot be worked out without one's being at the climax of spirituality—and this was Muhammad. After all, the whole prime of manhood spent in retirement in the Cave of Hirá could not remain without bringing its fruits. Though they were the early days of his marriage, Muhammad would often retire to the cave and spend month after month there in divine contemplation. There the angel of God appeared to him and brought him the first message.

His duties increased with his ministry, but nothing could keep him back from his communion with God, his days in action, but his nights in long prayers. Even in the busy life of Medina one could see his feet swelling, as for nights he was on them in the presence of God, and thus continued till he left the world.

A COMPARISON

> *"Religion cannot be said to have made a bad choice in pitching on this Man as the ideal representative and guide of humanity"* (Renan).

So the French philospher Renan (d. 1092 C.E.) remarked when speaking of Jesus. Renan, with all his rationalistic attainments, was no proof against his early predilection. A calm and unprejudiced consideration of what we read in the Bible as to the life of Jesus, in the light of what is necessary to constitute human society, will convince our readers that the remark of Renan was not free from short-sightedness. He should have known that there were various walks of life most necessary for the superstructure of human society, where Jesus Christ, as reported in the Evangelical record, could not be a guide. A king on the throne, a judge on the bench, a statesman in his cabinet, and general in the field, are as necessary units of human society as a teacher of morality; and God was also not unwise in raising patriarchs like David, Solomon, Joseph and Joshua, who acted respectively as a king, a minister of state and a general. They were human beings, and possibly committed errors in the performance of such duties. But if God had to come as the "ideal representative and guide of humanity," as it is said He did in the person of Jesus, we could have been more benefited if God had appeared as a king or a statesman. He could have left better rules for the guidance of Christian kings and statesmen in Europe, and the world have been saved the terrible conflagration of the last two world wars into which it has been thrown under ambition and selfassertiveness.

But Jesus was not for the world; he came only for something spiritual—some of our readers will think so when reading the above. I wish one could disillusion such friends of their wrong conception of spirituality. With them, perhaps, spirituality means effacement of mundane duties. But Jesus was not a recluse, after all. He was a man of action as well. To fast and to see visions, to pray away the midnight hours and to talk with God through the night watches, as Cardinal Newman wrongly thinks, is not the whole spirituality. "The weekday side of our life," in the words of J.R. Miller, D.D., "has a great deal more to do with the spiritual life, with the building of our character, with our growth in grace, than many of us think. On the other hand, no day can be made beautiful whose secular side is not so full and complete as its religious side." But what else is religious side? Where lies the dividing line between the religious and the secular, when you lead a life of purity and chastity, of charity and benevolence in all its walks? Are not our physical conditions closely connected with our moral and spiritual? Even our drinking and eating play a great part in the world of our moral and spiritual conditions. Jesus himself made no difference between what is called a secular and a religious life. It was, however, for Muhammad to bring so clearly home to the world that every act of a person "has a religious bearing, a religious significance; his whole life from the cradle to the grave is one series of religious performances. There is no sharp dividing line between religion and politics. There is no such thing as 'Render unto Caesar what is Caesar's and unto God what is God's, Caesar is but a representative of God, and obedience to him is obedience to God. Not only had he to regulate the ritual, frame religious ordinances, direct the worship of his followers, but he had also to guide their political destiny." And was Jesus a recluse, or a man of action? His life was one both of prayer and action. His nights he passed in communing with God; his mornings found him doing all sorts of good offices to those in need and distress. He was none the less spiritual when he was in the company of the publicans and tax-collectors. Did not his spiritual powers find their exhibition when he was participating in a marriage ceremony? And if the weekday side of his life was quite consistent with his spirituality, Jesus could not have become less spiritual if he had been raised as a king or a potentate.

SPIRITUALITY OF MUHAMMAD IN DAILY LIFE

And if spirituality consist chiefly in doing something to advance real human happiness by precept and example, a king is also advanced in spirituality, for he can do more to further human happiness than a discarded recluse. Humility of mind and meekness in deportment, the two among several other essentials of spirituality, when exhibited by those who can afford to do otherwise, add charms to their owner. They are taken as a good moral object-lesson and act as a magic wand converting every haughty, stiff-necked person into a gentle and humble creature. But when these high morals find their manifestation in one humble in position, they only invite effrontery and rebuke and excite jeer and jest. They are not taken as good morals of their owner, but as a necessary outcome of his low social status.

And in this respect Muhammad is the only glorious illustration of true spirituality.

Once an orphan, again a persecuted citizen, again one flying for his life, and then a spiritual and temporal chief. But could this taste of power change his method of living? Did he surround himself with the pomp of power? Did he keep a retinue or bodyguard, or did he indulge in any one of those outward manifestations of earthly glory in which the monarchs of the earth, ancient and modern, have loved to clothe themselves? Did he amass wealth or leave a large fortune behind? In fact, in no one single respect did he change. Power, notwithstanding, and stupendous power too, for he exercised a power which the greatest of monarchs might have envied, he remained to the last simple, unostentatious, free from pride, living for his flock and living with them with a self-sacrifice rarely to be seen in life. Here is the *great potentate,* but *"poor in spirit"*. Here is the great builder of temporal and religious power, but meek, merciful and pure in heart, who inherited "the earth but did hunger and thirst after righteousness." In his case upwards became reality and actions. This is real spirituality, which remains, unflinching, and unscathed, even in affluence and prosperity. One who is meek and humble in poverty and adversity has nothing to lose if he chooses to be so; but he has still to put his spirituality to test if he dips deep into the well of riches and power and remains unaffected. I will refer here to the tribute paid by a German scholar, Dr. Gustav Weil, to Muhammad:

"Muhammad set a shining example to his people. His character was pure and stainless. His dress, his food, they were characterized by a rare simplicity. So unpretentious was he that he would receive from his companions no special mark of reverence, nor would he accept any service from his slave which he could do himself. Often and often was he seen in the market purchasing provisions; often and often was he seen mending his clothes in his room, or milking a goat in his courtyard. He was accessible to all and at all times. He visited the sick and was full of sympathy for all. Unlimited was his benevolence and generosity, and so was his anxious care for the welfare of the community. Despite innumerable presents which from all quarters unceasingly poured in for him, he left very little behind, and even that he regarded as state property."

MAGNANIMITY OF THE PROPHET MUHAMMAD

Take, again, his triumphal entry into Mecca. What a glorious instance of forbearance! Arabia lay prostrate at his feet and Mecca, the stronghold of opposition, was entirely at his mercy. Did he then show a spirit of revenge? And could he not, if he had so willed, have cut off the head of every one there, those implacable enemies of his who gave him no quarter, who forced him to leave his native land to seek shelter, who held him up to scorn and ridicule, who persecuted him with rancour and bitterness which was at once cruel and unreasonable?

But the personal element never entered into his actions at all. He rejected every token of personal homage and declined all regal authority, and when the haughty chiefs of the Quraysh appeared before him he asked:

"What can you expect at my hands?"

"Mercy, O generous brother!"

"Be it so, you are free."

His simplicity, his humanity, his frugality, his forbearance, his earnestness, his steadfastness, his firmness in adversity, his meekness in power, his humility in greatness, his anxious care for animals, his passionate love for children, his unbending sense of fairness and justice!—Is there another instance in the history of the world where we have the assemblage of all these virtues woven into one character?

After centuries of perversion of facts and suppression of truth, the figure of Muhammad stands aloft to-day compelling the admiration and commanding the reverence of the non-Muslim world. He is no longer an impostor, but a great reformer. He is no longer a neurotic patient suffering from epilepsy, but a man of tremendous character and unbending will. He is no longer a self-seeking despot, ministering to his own selfish ends, but a beneficent ruler shedding light and love around him. He is no longer an opportunist, but a Prophet with a fixed purpose, undeviating in his constancy. All this Europe has now acknowledged, and acknowledged freely. We have the appreciative works of Higgins, Davenport, Bosworth, Smith and Carlyle in English; of Krehl and Grimme in German; the monumental work of Caetani in Italian. There are others besides, scholarly works. It is true, but they are not altogether free from those prejudices which at one time constituted the stock-in-trade of Christendom.

"SERMON ON THE MOUNT" NO GUIDE TO HUMANITY

The deeper I go into the question, the more doubtful. I become as to the correctness of Renan's remark given above. The morality taught by Jesus in his Sermon on the Mount never found favour even with his immediate followers. The precepts in the sermon may be taken as an idealism, but the world for the last two thousand years could not see its way to bring them into practice. Even the devout workers of his mission find themselves often unfit to work out these idealistic principles of ethics, and are only waiting for the second advent of Christ when the Kingdom of heaven shall come to restore peace, amity, and love, and man, becoming circumcised of all stern but otherwise manly passions, will be in a more suitable disposition to act upon them. We may accept this apologetic exposition: but what about the stern side of our character, which, dangerous as it seemingly appears to peace, is also an essential factor in maintaining the same? Jesus may guide us in the exercise of our tender passive moral qualities, but happiness to human society greatly depends also upon the exercise of the stern ones when properly secure. One may brand them as lower passions; but is it not just an act of godliness if we hate falsehood, if we are angry with anything cruel or wrong, and if a culprit is brought to book and society is avenged in the interest of public safety? These passions have their right use, and it is only in their degenerate use that they become bestial. On the other hand, they become higher morality when they are put to their proper use. To say these stern passions are undesirable is simply to find fault with the Supreme Wisdom. Are not hatred and anger relatives? Do they not affect the trend of human affairs? And if man is born in the image of God, all the moral qualities, tender or stern, observable in him must be divine moral attributes in man, and they cannot be dispensed with. Do we not observe them in the working of dumb nature, the best index of divine character; do we not read of them in the Bible as attributes of God?—and if we exercise them we simply go after God. These passions no doubt require regulation and training, and it is in the life of a perfect man in whom God is claimed to have been revealed that we look for the right use of such passions. Is not the get-your-both-cheeks-struck morality sufficient, if adopted, to destroy those stern morals which are divine, and to render our life and property insecure? Is not the resist-not-evil principle of life a premium to cruelty and rowdyism? This kind of morality seems to be too high-flown to be practiced, and will remain so till the day judgment. But can the Teacher of the Sermon on the Mount under these conditions claim to be a perfect model of humanity and an ideal representative of mankind as Renan makes him to be? But leaving apart anger, hatred and vengeance, there are other moral attributes besides those claimed as Christian morals observable in us. Modesty meekness, and patience do no exhaust the long list of human morals. Bravery, justice, chivalry, generosity, self-confidence and many other noble qualities—they did hardly find their exhibition in actions in the record of Jesus. To take the most favourable view of the case,, Jesus a great Divine Messenger, possessed them potentially; but they remained in abeyance, and did not see their revelation in him, as he did not get the occasion necessary for the manifestation of these morals.

MUHAMMAD—A PERFECT SPECIMEN IN PRACTICE

A possible potentially is no proof of actuality, and negative virtues are not virtues, especially in teachers of morality. They cost nothing, and are no help to one who needs a specimen in practice. You may read homilies of forgiveness and sermons of meekness, but lip-teachings are no proof of their possession by you. Words converted into actions only can justify our claims to possession. How can you teach lessons of patience and meekness if you never happened to face the hardest trials of life as Jesus did? What a marvelous thing to find the Teacher of Islam as just up to our demand! From orphanage to kingship Muhammad passed through different stages of life. Events of diverse nature arose in his life which demanded manifestation of various characters. At every step he was weighed, but was never found wanting. We need a perfect model up to our needs in several walks of life, and the life of the Prophet Muhammad eloquently promises it in itself. A king, a statesman, a warrior, a general, a lawgiver, a judge, a tradesman, a friend, a father, a son, a husband, a neighbour—all these characters are mirrored in most beautiful colours in the life of the Prophet; and it is not through his sermons and teachings that we have to make an estimate of him and to learn morals from him, but through actions and deeds.

MUHAMMAD—A TEACHER THROUGH ACTION

And in this lies the superiority of the Great Prophet of Islam over the prophets of the world. They leave us legacies of words, though of wisdom and guidance; but for their translation into actions we look in vain in the account of these teachers' lives. Teachings put into practice by the teacher himself are our need. It will help us to appreciate them and guide us to act upon them. But, unfortunately, what we know of these teachers is too meager to guarantee it. They are not even historic.

THE HISTORIC PROPHET

They are enshrouded in obscurity. Their life smacks of something strange and antique. They speak like oracles, and even the few words reported to have escaped from their lips hardly enable us to have an insight into their character. The Prophet Muhammad on the other hand, is more historic than Caesar and Alexander the Great. His life is just like a mirror before us where different characters of high-mindedness, generosity, bravery, patience, meekness, forgiveness, and other necessary constituents of humanity reflect in most brilliant colours. The life of the Prophet is an eloquent commentary of the sacred Book. Every virtue recommended or any vice enjoined against in the Qur'án, and the same you will find illustrated in the actions of the Prophet. The importance of it can hardly be exaggerated. Without it we are unable to appreciate one's teaching and we give it up as hopeless, but for our regard for the teacher we sometimes call it as something ideal, which really means an impracticability. "Love your enemy" did not pass beyond the domain of dream in Christianity, but Muhammad has shown us how love for the enemy may be shown in practice. Only a practical benefactor of humanity like Muhammad could say: "For the love of God give away your wealth in freeing those enemies whom you have captured in war." So was enjoined in the Qur'án, and so in every case Muhammad acted upon the injunction, and the

Muslim conquerors in the footsteps of their Master always spent their wealth in freeing their captives. Similarly everything in the Qur'án found its practical illustration in the life of the Teacher. His life was eventful, and furnished him occasions to manifest what was noble and good in him. It is due to the extreme opulence of the life of the Prophet in practical demonstration of all the many virtues that we recognize in him the most perfect figure in the history of man.

MUHAMMAD IN ADVERSITY THE DIVERSIFICATION OF INDUSTRY

In fact, one who could not experience change in the circumstances of his life cannot afford to be a perfect model for others' imitation. Every moral quality requires given conditions, and unless they are present one cannot be rightly accredited with it. Adversity and prosperity are necessary to give revelation to different moralities. Trial gives man a character, but success brings forth his nobility of mind if he possesses it. In fact, humanity is not only softness of heart. It consists of various morals, tender and stern, and they need variety of conditions for their development. If some find manifestation in penury, others demand affluence for perfection. Very few guides of humanity were given an occasion to taste both. But Muhammad, to act as a perfect model for humanity, had to pass through every phase of life, if prosperity brings forth his generosity, his forgiveness and his high-mindedness, his adversity gives him an occasion to exhibit his patience, fortitude, and his trust in God.

Reference

1. See *Encyclopaedia Britannica*, eleventh edition; art, "Koran."

[***By:*** *—Khwaja Kamal-ud-Din*
Source: *The Islamic Review & Arab Affairs, July–August 1970.*]

6

Charges Against the Prophet of Islam Refuted

It is well that all should know how Christendom has treated, and is still treating Islam and its Prophet. If I were to begin at the beginning and recount the whole story of Christianity's vituperative propaganda against Islam, together with its concoction and distortion of facts for the belittlement of Islam in the eyes of the world, I should fill volumes over volumes. In spite of his so-called Orientalism and Oriental studies, all that the average Christian's conception of Islam is, of a religion of horror, cruelty and intolerance in public life, of polygamy, easy divorce, and licentiousness in private,— and this because, through religious instruction imparted in schools and sermons broadcast from pulpit, press and platform, Christian teachers and ministers have all along been telling their fold that Islam is, just than this, lest the sheep be tempted to stray into the dens of the wolves. Even in the field of history, when Christian writers take up the pen to write Muslim history, they twist historical events to suit their own dishonest purpose, and, not content with mere distortion of facts, they brazenly draw conclusions, however wrong and remote they may be, from the facts so distorted, and pass them on as the result of scientific investigation and scholarly research. We shall not be justified in blaming or upbraiding them if their allegations were to be attributed to ignorance, but such is not the case, for with full cognizance of the truth they deliberately conceal it or present it in such a way as to make of Islam a horror, and of its Prophet a sham leader and a selfish man. The duty of a historian is only to record events faithfully, not to pass judgment on them, or to find the why's and wherefore's of this one or that. The right to pass judgment on an event and to criticise it in the light of facts and according to the principles of ethics, is that of the philosopher and the moralist; but these self-styled historians have given whatever reasons and causes have appealed to them for events Islamic, for, alas, there is hardly a European writer who is not biased, or who has been faithful in recording Muslim events. Nay, in many instances these writers have drawn on their invention as best might serve their purpose, and have dressed up the results in the disguise of real historical events.

Let me give an example. A certain Christian writer says that the Prophet of Islam had a pet pigeon, which he trained so that it would come and sit on his shoulder when called, and pick the grain from his ear. This the Prophet would do, according to this writer, to deceive people into believing that the angel in the form of the bird was coming to him to reveal the word of God. It would appear at first sight that the author has at least taken this alleged occurrence from some reliable source, and afterwards, it may be, added his own opinion on the subject, but the truth is that there is no event whatsoever of this nature in the life of the Holy Prophet. What seems to have happened is that there was in the author's mind the event of the Holy Ghost coming to Jesus in the form of a dove. He thought that some similar phenomenon must have happened to our Prophet, but inasmuch as he believed our Prophet to be a false prophet he attempted to prove it so by introducing a purely imaginary story about the pet bird and its training.

It is lamentable to see men of education taking events from the life of the one person and fathering them on to another, adding at the same time their own fabrications so as to paint the latter in the blackest hues. The mischief fulfils its purpose. Many readers are confused, and if any be a non-Muslim they are, as often as not, convinced. Thus the ball is set a-rolling and another writer of the same kidney will quote such fictions by way of authority, because they will believe anything that goes against Islam and its Prophet. All sense of fair play is forgotten when they write about Islam. I have given one instance of this, but here is another.

A Christian writer says that the Prophet was subject to fits of epilepsy, and that each time he had an attack, he would pretend that he was receiving revelation. Now there could be nothing more absurd than such an allegation, because this able author in his zeal to defame the Prophet, has written something which neither the external facts nor medical opinion can support. He has no authority to cite in this contention, that Prophet had ever been a victim to epilepsy. Such a thing would soon have been found out by the Qureish who were his enemies, and they would have eagerly utilized it as a weapon to put an end to him and his preachings. History tells us that the Arabs did all in their power to end his career, but even to them it never occurred to frame such a particular charge. And why? Because they knew that it was not a fact and would not be worth the attempt. As to epileptic fits, Ostler in his *Practice of Medicine* writes: —

> After the attack the patient may be dazed a few seconds, and perform certain automatic actions which may seem to be rotational. As mentioned, undressing is a common action, but all sorts of odd actions may be performed.

None of these symptoms could ever be traced in the Prophet. Epileptic fits are the results of a sick brain, the victim of which becomes irritable, cowardly, irresolute, exhausted and dull, suffering indeed from general debility. The colour of such a person becomes pale, and his blood thin. Now whoever has read his life of the Prophet, even as told by Christian writers, cannot say that he suffered from any of these weaknesses of body or mind. On the contrary, the accounts of his life, all go to show that he was brave, active, alert, sagacious and possessed of the best of health. If he had been subject to epileptic fits he could never have achieved, as he did, the greatest success of which a man is capable. To bring a social and moral revolution to a successful termination; to change the people's outlook of things from the bestial and depressing to the human and bright; to subdue a fighting, ignorant, wild and idolatrous race by moral force and argument—all this cannot surely be achieved by a diseased brain. All his words and deeds show that he possessed an extraordinarily healthy brain, which could foster a complete scheme for the salvation of the world, and see it successfully worked out to the end. He was active as no other man has ever been. His foresight can never be equalled. It is, therefore, inconceivable that he could be subject to the disease from which he is alleged to have been suffering. The sayings and words of wisdom which came from him and the prophecies he uttered, and their miraculous fulfilment, some of them after the lapse of ages, can never have been the product of a sickly brain.

Now, allegations such as these are nothing but dishonest propaganda against the Prophet. One is inclined to think, as I have said, that the allegations themselves are the outcome of a diseased brain, for no sane person could have ever dreamed of writing such palpable untruths against such a benefactor to humanity. What is most painful in this connection is that these are not stray cases, but common amongst those entrusted with the task of preaching the gospel of love and charity.

I would, therefore, request all fair-minded people to take whatever these Christian writers say about Islam and its Prophet not only with just a pinch, but a big pinch of salt.

[***By:*** *—Muhammad Ali Al-Haj Salmin*

Source: *The Islamic Review*]

7

The Moral Aspect of the Life of the Holy Prophet Muhammad

A speech delivered at a reception held in honour of the memory of the Holy Prophet: —

Ladies and Gentleman and you especially, my Brothers and Sister in Islam! I welcome you here to-night when we are gathered to honour the memory of the Great Arabian Prophet and celebrate the anniversary of his birth. You have heard that I was privileged a few months ago to visit the Sacred Places of Islam and do the pilgrimage to Mecca, the city where Muhammad was born and where he lived the first 40 years of his life, esteemed and honoured by his fellow-citizens who gave him the title of *Al-Amin*, because he was known never to break his promise, or do a mean action, or tell a lie, or let down a friend. He always had a smile for the little children he loved, and a helping hand for those in need. Muhammad felt deeply the degradation of his people who were sunk in idolatry and superstition, offering human sacrifices, burying their unwanted female babies alive, and doing other unnameable atrocities. In those days Muhammad was wont to retire to a lonely cave situated in the barren hills that surround Mecca, and in this cave he spent long hours and days and even weeks, in prayer and contemplation and it was in this cave—the Cave of Hira—that he first realized that he was divinely inspired and that he had a message for humanity.

It must have been hard to his sensitive mind, to leave his quiet, well-ordered life and plunge into the strife and bitter recrimination that he felt would ensue, when he called on the tribes to forsake their idols and worship God alone. He knew that his own relations, the Quraish, would be among his worst enemies, as they had been for over 700 years hereditary guardians of the idols in the Kaaba and had a vested interest in the old worship. At first the Holy Prophet opened his soul only to his wife, Khadijah, who became his first convert and to a few of his intimate friends, but on receiving a further Divine Command to preach the Truth to all men, Muhammad, overcoming his diffidence, called on his fellow-citizens to assemble on the hill of Safa, where he addressed them in the following words (I propose to read to you because, though they have lost somewhat their beauty and force through the translation from the original Arabic, I think you will still find them beautiful): "Oh ye children of the Mighty One! Do you take me to be true or false? If ye consider me to be true, will you hearten to what I say? The caravan of our life will one day surely depart hence. Beware ye of the time when death shall attack. All in their turn will leave you, whether it be your relation or belongings. If there be any bliss remaining with you, it is the good which ye have done in your life. God alone is worthy of praise. His name is worthy of repetition. His thought is worthy of contemplation; His command is worthy of obedience and His majesty is worthy of service. When ye think, think only of Him; when ye bow, bow only before Him; trust Him alone, fear Him alone, and serve Him alone. No one lives outside of Him, none can be compared with Him. The wise and the foolish are both speechless before Him. The sun and the moon are motionless in His presence. Mighty Kings are submissive before His Exalted Majesty. The righteous and the pious are absorbed in His Presence. Neither the hermit nor the orthodox has any power in His Kingdom. Neither the ascetic nor the mystic has a voice in His Court. Therefore count not on a mediator between you and your God."

The storm of anger that followed this public announcement forced the Prophet to discontinue, and he was shouted at and called a madman. Cruel abuse and satire was hurdled at him when he showed himself in the streets of the city. But inspired by the knowledge of his Divine Message he continued to preach from the street corners, the market place, and the hills and he gained many converts. When he found he could not protect his disciples, most of whom suffered martyrdom, he advised them to emigrate with their families to Abyssinia and Medina, while he himself remained on at his post. But after a time, finding his life was in danger, he fled with one faithful friend Abu Baker to Medina, where he received a warm welcome from the Muslims already gathered there. But there was no peace for Muhammad in Medina; it was an endless *Jihad,* striving of good against evil, until after ten long years the good prevailed. Idolatory was overcome and the Arabs of the great peninsula embraced Islam. The Prophet returned to his native city, Mecca, in triumph. He was virtually king of Arabia, with rulers of neighbouring kingdoms seeking his friendship. But he refused the pomp and pageantry of kingship and return to his little house in Medina, where, when not immersed in affairs of State, he continued to live his former simple life subsisting generally on dates and camel's milk.

But the long years of hardship had told on the prophet—thirteen years of cruel persecution in Mecca, followed by 10 years of ceaseless *Jihad* in Medina. And now feeling his end near, he called on his disciples to carry on his work, urging tolerance: "Let there be no compulsion in religion,"[1] and enjoining on them the necessity of acquiring knowledge for "the ink of the scholar is more precious than the blood of the martyr;" "Acquire knowledge—it enableth its possessor to distinguish right from wrong, it lighteth the path to heaven, it is our friend in the desert, our society in solitude, our comrade when friendless, it guideth to happiness, it sustaineth in adversity, it is an ornament among friends and armour against enemies."

The mission of the Prophet was accomplished and his intrepid spirit took flight to the blessed companionship above, and thus ended a life devoted to God and humanity. His disciples fired by his example carried the faith of Islam not only through Asia but to Egypt, through Northern Africa, Spain and Southern Europe, establishing universities, mosques, hospitals and schools of learning in the cities, holding the flame of their Faith and the torch of civilization to a darkened Europe sunk in ignorance and superstition.

Muhammad was the greatest prophet and the greatest legislator the world has ever seen, and for us Muslims to whom has descended the heritage of his example and the glorious Qur-án, it is for us to try and follow in his footsteps and live the life he would have us live, holding to our faith and who knows that one day Islam may help to heal the wounds of humanity.

Reference

1. The Qur'án Chap. II.

[*By:* —*The Lady Evenly Cobbold.*
Source: *The Islamic Review*]

8

Was the Prophet Muhammad Harsh to the Jews?

Nissim Rejwan, Jewish writer, in an article, "Judeo-Arabic Civilisation" in *Work,* Tel Aviv, for November 1966, has made an unwarrantable statement in an otherwise lucid, eloquent and well-informed piece of writing. Nissim Rejwan says:

> "For when he discovered that the Jews refused to accept him, Mohammad turned his fury against them and proceeded to persecute and expel them from Arabia."

However, one must agree with the learned author that the period from the commencement of Islam's popularity in Medina to the expulsion of the Jews from Khaybar during the Caliphate of Umar, was a "brief period of rift and hostility" but to find out the bases thereof, one should have taken the trouble of reading the Islamic history and the invaluable stock of research piled up by the scholars of the past. The writer proposes to deal with the subject regarding the Prophet's treatment of the Hebrew community in two parts historical and observational. The historical aspect of the Judeo-Islamic (*not Judeo-Arabic)* relations during the Prophet's time has been dealt with first. The observational section is based on some general remarks, supported by the Holy Qur'án Bible and the Sayings of the Prophet Muhammad himself.

HISTORICAL

An Introduction to the Jews

The real known history of the Jews begins with their seldom under the tyrannical Pharaohs. God raised Moses from among themselves and they were brought "out of the land of Egypt, out of the house of bondage." Soon after they entered a Covenant with the Lord through Moses, and it was as a result of honouring its terms that they witnessed eras of peace and plenty. They got a land to live in and they carved it into two small states of Judah and Samaria.

After Moses, the Jews did not stick to what he had taught. Hence they were suppressed twice, once by the Babylonians in 587 B.C., and for the second time by Vespasian's son in 70 C.E. Their temple and towns were destroyed, their men and women butchered and taken into captivity. Their beautiful females were taken by the Roman victors.

The desolation of the states of the children of Israel had already been predicted by their apostles, namely, Isaiah, Jeremiah and Jesus. All of them detested and despised the Jewish way of life prevalent then. Conveying to them the displeasure of God, these apostles warned the people but to no avail. At the time of Muhammad's preaching the message, the Jews were scattered, living a rebellious life.

Long before the advent of Islam into Medina, the Jews had established themselves at the fertile places of Khaybar and in the suburbs of Yathrib (later called Medina). There they formed a potent element and a considerable power. Trade coupled with usury had made them rich. They owned land and controlled local markets. Enjoying at the time social and cultural superiority, they managed their own institutions of education and religious endownments. By various means they even won converts from the Arabs. The "purity" of their race could not be, therefore, maintained in Arabian conditions. The Jews in Arabia bore Arab names and lived like the Arabs.

With the passage of time, the Jews had developed innumerable social defects and become quite endemic.

Increasingly prosperous, they had succumbed to various social evils. Their relations with others. They had become naughty. They subjected their debtors to unjust treatment, keeping their belongings, children and even wives as pawns, and imposed exhorbitant rates of interest. Shakespeare only reveals the truth about an average Jew of that period, when he puts these words in the mouth of the Duke in the *Merchant of Venice:*

> *"I am sorry for thee (Antonio): thou art come to answer a stony adversary (Shylock), an inhuman wretch incapable of pity, void and empty from any dram of mercy."*

This was true of the ancient Jews, with exceptions, of course. And this was true. More or less, of the later Jews in Europe and West Asia. Hence their proscription in the mediaeval age. Thus in Christendom they were hated "for foul usure, and lucre of vilanie."

THE COVENANT WITH THE JEWS AND ITS PROMINENT FEATURES

Arrival of the Prophet and Agreements with the Jews

Before the Prophet of Islam reached Medina, the polytheists and the Jews had proposed to install 'Abdullah Ibn Ubayy as the ruler in the hope of forming a good government. This proposal was, however, withdrawn on Muhammad's arrival, for the local people considered him to be the most appropriate person to take on the responsibility of administering the affairs of the town and the surrounding territory.

The Prophet perceived that both the internal situation of the town and the antagonism of the Quraysh towards Islam necessitated the establishment of a concord between the Jews and the tribes of Aws and Khazraj, most of whom had become Muslims. The practice of making agreements was not quite new to these people. The Jews "used to enter into alliance with the tribes and to take part in their internecine warfare." Notwithstanding this, it was an achievement of the Prophet to have found a common basis for an accord, called a Charter or Covenant in history. The Holy Qur'án (2:84) refers to it thus:

> *"And when we made a covenant with you (to this effect): Shed no blood amongst you, nor turn out your own people from your homes: and this ye solemnly ratified, and to this ye can bear witness."*

The Covenant is divisible into three parts. The first defines the position of the Muslims themselves and organizes them into a religious and socio-civic unity; the second provides a political arrangement to which the Jews too became a part and to whom it was acceptable; the third binds the parties to work together for the defence of Medina and also extends security to all the peoples living in an area of a hundred square miles.

The Allies of the covenantees were thus transformed into a political union of which there was no example in past history. Medina was recognized as being vital to the Muslim brotherhood and its territory was regarded as the "forbidden one." The Jews, who after the victory of Badr became conscious of their isolation and weakness and who joined the alliance soon after, were to enjoy equal rights with others. Politically more significant sounds the fact that all the parties had recognized the Prophet of Islam as the last court of appeal in the event of murder or a difference arising amongst them.

A remarkable feature of the covenant was that the parties undertook to be loyal to the "Central Authority." It imposed joint and separate duty on the signatories for the protection of Medina. In the case of external aggression and making of peace and war, they were to stand as one. No one was to fight (if the cause was common) without the prior permission of the prophet. The expenses of war were to be borne by the party at war. In practising their religion, the Jews were completely free.

The fact that the covenant was binding on all meant that no party or clan could dissent or dissociate itself when it lied: no one among the signatories or their members could break the terms agreed upon.

A city-state had thus been given birth to by a solemn contract, which was consciously made and of which the terms were inviolable. A wilful attempt to bring about the dissolution of the new political party was, therefore, to be deemed an act of treason.

Judeo-Islamic Differences Increase

Meanwhile, the Prophet continued to preach social reform. Also, he *peacefully* propagated the tenets of Islam. As a result, the number of admissions to the faith multiplied. The popularity of Islam awakened the Jews to the loss of their influence which they had founded on materialism and not the true Mosaic Law. Above all, they seem to have been deprived of the future converts; for the Prophet had brought with him superior moral values and a just and generous treatment of the non-believing sections. Thus further Judaization of the Arabians had come to a standstill.

Nothing could deter or divert the Prophet of Islam from preaching the eradication of immorality and corruption. In doing so, he was not acting detrimentally to the terms of the covenant. The Jews had acquired full liberty to exercise the religion that the prophet Moses and his successors had preached. The revelations received by the Prophet Muhammad pointing to the evils of the Jewish society most have displeased the Banu Israel. These are referred to in the Qur'an:

> *"That they took usury, though they were forbidden and that they devoured men's property wrongfully..." (4:160).*
>
> *"Many of them dost thou see, racing each other in sin and rancour, and their eating of things forbidden..." (5:62).*
>
> *"In (they are fond of) listening to falsehood, of devouring anything forbidden" (7:63).*

From these verses it would appear that the Jews suffered from certain moral ailments such as greed that made them stick to usury and devour property or things of others which they were forbidden to do; their sinful life and their virulence, which suppressed their very soul; and their listening to falsehood against the true facts about Islam and the Last Messenger.

Under such circumstances, it is not surprising that the Jews tried to interrupt the peaceful development of the Islamic movement. They resorted to ingenious method in order to injure Muhammad's work and the Muslim brotherhood. Some of these were asking him to cause a book to be descended from God, while they had asked Moses for a greater miracle, e.g., "Show us God in public"; embracing the Muslim faith with the set purpose of creating trouble from within; encouraging desertions from the ranks of Islam; teasing the Prophet Muhammad in a provocative manner; inviting him to converse with the Jewish doctors of law with the apparent aim of accepting Islam; making attempts to assassinate him; remaining in touch with the enemies of Islam such as Ibn Ubayy; and lastly, bringing to the Prophet their knotty problems and disputes dishonestly, so that in the event of misjudgment, they might inform the world that Muhammad's faith and system lacked the Divine basis.

In spite of the repugnant and rebellious attitude of the Jews, the Prophet adhered to a persevering and peaceful policy and wished that the Judaic prestige be maintained. This he did because of his awareness of the fact that he had spiritual links with the Prophet Moses. Not only did he emphasize similarities between him and Moses, not in many points followed what God had approved of through the latter. In particular, where the Qur'án was silent or where a revelation from God had not been received, Muhammad would take assistance from the Mosaic practice. It was for these reasons that he would appeal to the Jews to agree and collaborate with the Muslims. For this purpose God enjoined him to approach the Hebrews (and Christians) and say:

> *"O People of the Book! Come to common terms as between us and you; that we worship none but God; that we associate no partners with Him, that we erect not, from among ourselves, lords and patrons other than God ..." (The Qur'án, 4:63).*

Thus Muhammad was simply inviting the Jews to the propositions that were common between them and the

Muslims, leaving the two people free in other matters. Also, this should bring home the truth that the Prophet of Islam was not basically saying anything that ran counter to what the Prophet Moses had taught. The Qur'ánic evidence further strengthens the Prophet's position in that many well-meaning Jews approved of his teachings. As for the fact that he preached the eradication of social evils and the discarding of questionable means of livelihood, no sensible man among the Jews could controvert him and his companions.

HOSTILITIES AND THE JEWISH EXPULSION

Cast in the mould of antagonism, the Jews as a community had decided upon assuming an overbearing attitude towards Muhammad and his followers. The first to confront Islam were the Qaynuqá' and the Nadir—the two Jewish tribes. They were permitted to leave and settle beyond the "forbidden territory" of Medina. As for the third tribe, the Banu Quraydah, it was convicted of the treason committed during the battle of Ahzab. About 300 men of this tribe were executed. A brief description of the mutual dealings of the Jews and the Muslims seems essential to the understanding of the subject under review.

1. The Tribe of Qaynuqá'

After Islam had emerged victorious from the battlefield of Badr, the first among the Jews to have apprehensions as to what their future would be were the Qaynuqá'. Lacking coolness of temperament, they acted in a manner as to lead to the estrangement of the Muslim feelings. Their jealousy grew into enmity. "Insinuations against Muslim ladies in obscene verses were also freely indulged in. They stooped so now as to molest them in the streets." Meanwhile, a Jewish shopkeeper added fuel to the fire when he offended a Muslim woman, resulting in the death of a Jew and a Muslim. The Prophet admonished the Jews but they responded by rude behaviour and warned the Muslims that they would teach them a good lesson. Discarding the terms of the covenant, they betook themselves to fortified places. The Muslims besieged them for two weeks and obliged them to surrender. The Qaynuqá' were then allowed to leave and settle elsewhere.

2. The Tribe of Nadir

The tribesmen of the Nadir looked at the rise of Islam with extreme disfavour. They adopted different devices to harm the interests of both the Islamic movement and its leader. Once Muhammad went to demand from them the blood-money, the remission of which they had undertaken. While he waited on them, the Nadir sent up a man to drop a stone on him from a house-top. Similarly, they pretended twice to accept Islam and invited the Prophet to hold a conversation with the scholars to Judaism. On both occasions the aim was to kill him, but he was saved because of being informed beforehand.

The Nadir joined a conspiracy and went down to Mecca, telling the Quraysh, "If you lend us support against Islam, we shall uproot it altogether." Besides rousing the Meccans, they roamed about the desert, visiting the haunts of the Bedouins and stirring them against Islam. The Nadir also remained in close touch with Ibn Ubayy, who encouraged them in their hostile designs.

When approached by the Muslims for renewing the old agreement, the Nadir refused to do so. This showed that they harboured evil intentions against Islam. Accordingly, when they fortified themselves within their strongholds, the Muslims laid siege to their abodes for a number of days. The Jews surrendered on the condition that they would be permitted to leave the territory of Medina. Taking with them their full camel loads, the Nadir put on arms and dressed themselves in finer garments and left in procession as if celebrating a festival.

Dr. Prideaux opines that the Prophet ordered a party of his men to pursue the emigrants and that they were all put to death. This is an allegation that has no foundation whatsoever. On the other hand, the translator of the Qur'án, George Sale, holds that the "incident from which Dr. Prideaux draws this strange conclusion relates really to the murder in cold blood of seventy Muslims, who, being invited to preach Islam, were treacherously put to death by an Arab tribe", i.e., their inviters. This charge is further disproved by the Prophet's disallowing the Ansár to withhold their Judaized sons from proceeding with the Jews. Justifying his disapproval, he expressed what God had revealed to him on the point:

> *"Let there be no compulsion in religion: Truth stands out clear from Error: whoever rejects evil and believes in God hath grasped the most trustworthy handhold that never breaks ..." (The Qur-án, 2:256).*

The expulsion of the Nadír, therefore, was not without strong reasons. "Islam, it must be borne in mind, was at this time passing through a very critical stage. It was the period of the battle of Uhud, when the enemies were on all sides up in arms to strike a deathblow at the faith." Hence the treatment meted out to these turbulent Jews.

3. The Banú Qurayzah

It was during the Battle of Ahzab that the Qurayzah, the last tribe of the Jews that had an alliance with the Muslims, turned out to be perfidious. When the "Confederates" (the Quraysh, the Nadir, the Ghatafan and the Bedouins) were knocking at the doors of Medina. Huayy Ibn Akhtab of the banished Nadir approached ka'b Ibn Asad, the chief of the Qurayzah, and won him and his men by his eloquence and assurance that Islam was on its last legs. At first, Ka'b had rejected the invitation on the ground that he had "always found Muhammad true to his word; to be perfidious to him will be against manliness." But later, the Qurayzah informed the Muslims: "We do not know who Muhammad is, and what the agreement was like." This attitude pointed to their decision to join the confederates in their effort to undermine Islam.

The view that the Qurayzah had a secret agreement with the enemies of Islam and that they were actively hostile at the Battle of Ahzáb is confirmed by the Holy Qur'án (33:26).

"And He drove down those of the People of the Book who backed them from their fortresses and He cast awe into their hearts; some you killed and you took some captive."

Sir William Muir admits that "it was agreed that the Qurayzah would assist the Quraysh", but he doubts as to the fact of their participation in the war. However, the agreement between them did not remain a dead letter. According to another writer, "it was agreed that as soon as the Confederates were able to force a passage across the Trench, the Jews would rise to attack the Muslim quarters, so that the Muslims would be caught between the Confederates in front and the Jews in the rear."

In pursuance of their plan, the Qurayzah sent a man to find out whether there were any soldiers inside the fortress that accommodated the Muslim families. It was, however, the chivalry of the old Safiyyah, the aunt of the Prophet, which saved the situation by killing the Jewish intruder and throwing his head off the gate. The Jews took a lesson from it and they abandoned the idea of attacking the stronghold. Nevertheless, the movements of the Jews caused a diversion in the Muslim effort against the Confederates, because they were required to depute 500 troops to protect the Muslim women. The treachery of the Qurayzah had, therefore, added enormously to the difficulties of the Muslims in the battlefield. They were, moreover, disappointed to see an ally entering into treaty relations with their enemy instead of repelling their attack as the agreement with the Muslims had provided.

When the coalition of the invaders disappeared from the battle arena, the Muslims were relieved of a great anxiety. The Confederates having failed in their attempt to crush Islam, the Prophet sent 'Alí to seek an explanation from the defaulters. The Qurayzah refused to do so and to surrender, and even used obscene language against the Prophet and his family. 'Alí reported the matter back to the Prophet, who ordered an advance to be made on the fastnesses of the Jews. According to him "to leave such an internal enemy unpunished would have been a source of ever-present danger to the safety of the Muslim community." The Qurayzah surrendered on the condition that Sa'd Ibn Mu'az became an arbitrator. Sa'd's finding was that the treachery in the hour of peril was a grave offence. He believed that it called for an exemplary punishment, in the absence of which solemn agreements could in future command little respect, and would be treated as worthless scraps of paper by any of the parties concerned. Hence he came to the conclusion that the punishment in no way milder than that prescribed for a vanquished foe in their own Scripture, the Old Testament, was their own desserts. This is what the Law of Moses lays down on the point:

"When you draw near to a city to fight against it, offer terms of peace to it. And if its answer to you is peace and it opens to you, then all the people who are found in it shall do forced labour for you and shall serve you. But if it makes no peace with you, but makes war against you, then you shall besiege it; and when the Lord your God gives it into your hands you shall put all its males to the sword, but the women and the little ones, the cattle, and everything else in the city, all its spoil, you shall take as booty for yourselves; and you shall enjoy the spoil of your enemies, which the Lord your God has given you..." (Deuteronomy, 20:10-14).

According to some scholars, this "severe" sentence the Jews had brought upon themselves, "first by their treachery, next by their resistance to the Muslims after they had been caught in their treachery, and finally by preferring the judgment of Sa'd, who had been their ally, rather than throwing themselves upon the well-known and oft-experienced mercy of the Prophet. The sentence was carried out but the Prophet invited intercession on behalf of the condemned, and in response to every plea of intercession, he remitted the sentence."

About 300 of the Qurayzah, chiefly the fighters were beheaded under the arbitration award. This treatment seemed justifiable for the reason that the Qurayzah had originally recognized themselves and the Muslims as *one people in* the covenant and had even renewed the agreement. But contrary to it, later they deserted their partners in the common cause in the hour of peril and thereby exposed them to jeopardy. The Qurayzah had, besides this, done many aggressive things which forced the Prophet to take drastic action against them.

4. Reduction of Khaybar

The Jews of Khaybar would have continued to live peacefully had the Huqayq families of the Nadír not resettled there. The riches and the resourcefulness of the Khaybarities stood in good stead to the banished Nadír when they expanded their area of intrigue and destructive activities. The malice of the Jews kept on growing in bitterness after the battle of Azhab. The apparently humiliating Peace of Hudaybiyyah deepened their impression as to the powerlessness of the Muslims. The Huqayq chiefs and their hosts, moreover, "found that their incitement of Arab tribes against the Prophet had, in view of the Treaty of Hudaybiyyah, little chance of success; therefore, they turned their attention to the Christian and Pagan tribes in the north, who were under the Byzantine Emperor, and they also started intriguing with the Jews settled in Iraq and with the Iranian Emperor. Thus, though the Prophet and the Muslims might have peace in South and Central Arabia, they were to be exposed to fresh and even greater dangers from the north and the north-east. To prevent the whole of that region from flaring up at once against the Muslims, the least that was necessary was to remove the Jews from Khaybar, because the place served as a dangerous spot as well as a centre of disaffection and incitement close to Medina.

Being convinced that the Jews were determined to create trouble, the Prophet decided to nip the evil in the bud by obliging them to accept the status of citizen-subjects of the Islamic state. He took with him 1,600 men, including 200 cavalrymen, with the primary idea of incorporating the community of Khaybar, with full autonomy allowed to it. When the Muslim army covered the distance and the Jewish abodes were visible, the Prophet prayed to God, he usually did on seeing a new locality for the first time.

"O God! we seek from You the betterment of this village, its residents and its belongings and of our own betterment and Your shelter against its evils."

The Prophet abhorred the use of force, but on finding the Jews ready to fight, he ordered a match against the six fortresses of Khaybar. Excepting the fortress of the Qumás hill, all the Jewish strongholds were captured. The Qumás being impregnable and properly manned, Abú Bakr not succeeded in having it invested. The responsibility of accomplishing the deed fell on 'Alí, whose eyes at the time were aching. While proceeding on his errand, he asked the Prophet if conversion of the Jews by force was desired. The Prophet did not approve of the idea. 'Alí at once came to grips with the commander of the fortress. Marhab by name, and cut him into two, and emerged from the terrible combat as the victor of the occasion. The Jews lost 93, while the Muslim casualties numbered only 15, the first being Mahmúd Ibn Maslamah, whom Kinanah killed by dropping a stone on him.

As the Jews gave in, the Prophet permitted them to possess and cultivate their lands provided they remitted half the annual produce as tribute to Medina. As agreed to by the owners, Ibn Rawáhah would go to Khaybar at the harvest time and make two piles of the crops, asking them to choose either of the two. Impressed by this kind of treatment, the Jews used to say: "The earth and skies stand because of this even-handed justice." Allowing the Jews to hold the title of their own lands was a generous gesture on the part of the Prophet of Islam, although he knew that they would not refrain from sedition. The view that the Muslims ejected the vanquished from their holdings is baseless. Nor is it true that they were exterminated from Khaybar in the Prophet's own time. Later, however, a portion of the Jewish landed property was occupied by the Muslims, owing to the extreme recalcitrance of the Jews. Similarly the Judaic community of Khaybar was exiled during the Caliphate of 'Umar, who had found them most inhuman.

After the hostilities were over, the Prophet Muhammad has shown remarkable leniency and liberality to the Jews of Khaybar. And this in spite of their attempt to kill him by mixing poison with the food served at a banquet. When asked to explain themselves, the Jews replied, "We mixed poison to find out if you were a true Prophet. It would not affect you if you were one; and if you were not, we would thereby rid ourselves of you." Again, once, when a famine was raging at Medina, the Prophet sent two of his companions to Khaybar to secure relief from the Jewish landowners. But one of them, 'Abdulláh Ibn Suhay1 (the other being Mahísah), was treacherously killed and his body thrown into a rivulet. When informed of the tragedy, the Prophet forgave the culprits and paid blood-money from the public treasury. In the first case, only Zaynab, who had dared to serve the poisonous food, was executed after Bishr Ibn Bará'a died as a result of the poison; for he had hastened to pick up things at the feast. This leniency and the great qualities of Muhammad disprove still another charge that is leveled against him: he is blamed for having branded Kinánah, one of the Jewish chiefs, on his breast, for not disclosing secrets about the hidden treasure of Khaybar. Facts, in the light of history, however, point to the fact that the critics aim at falsifying real history.

1. Cause and Effect Theory

> *"It may be that your Lord may (yet) show Mercy unto you; but if ye revert (to your sins) We shall revert (to Our punishments) and We have made Hell a prison for those who reject (all faith)" (The Qur'án, 17:8).*

The Holy Qur'án thus sets forth the history of Cause and Effect, which has been at work throughout the history of nations. Effect according to the *Mauláná* Abul Kalám is the shadow of the *deed* or *action* and follows closely at its heels. Since the termination of the mission of Moses, the Banú Israel (i.e., the Jews) fell twice as a result of their own conduct. God offered them His mercy through Muhammad again, but they rejected him as well as his message. Hence the revelation that the Divine Law of punishment would automatically come into force. In two words, the Lord settled the issue for all time to come. The Jews, being the ancient Covenantees, were, in the present case warned, "If ye revert (to your sins) We shall revert (to Our punishments)." That is, if they were to continue in their sins, God's punishment would also continue to visit them. The punishment in the Prophet's time amounted to their expulsion from a 100 mile territory that had been agreed as the *forbidden area*. As provided in the alliance with the Muslims, there could be no room for the promoters of perfidy and peacelessness.

2. The Biblical Record of the Jewish Defiance and Downfall

The above warning of the Qur'án points to a yet greater historical fact about the Jewish people: they had repeatedly ignored acting upon the teachings of Moses, rejected their prophets and reformers and even killed and attempted to kill some of them. Suffering as they were from a superiority complex, the Hebrews disregarded the very basis on which they could claim distinction. The common belief that they surpassed all other peoples had led them off the track: they never adhered to the Lord's commands whereby they could really become great. They did not have the foresight to think of the possible outcome of their socio-religious vagaries and weaknesses. However, their prophets alone could discern the downfall of the Banú Israel through the latter's aggressive designs and dishonest methods. Let us go through the pages of the Bible itself which presents a graphic picture of the deplorable state of the Jewish communities, only to show that in not minding the warnings of the prophets they had proved that there was something basically wrong with their very nature. Here are their own prophets who frequently denounced the legatees of Moses and forewarned them as to the consequences.

Psalm 106 of David points to the recalcitrance and iniquity of the Banú Israel:

"Many times He delievered them, but they were rebellious in their purposes, and were brought low through their iniquity."

The Prophet Isaiah was dismayed as he found himself among the iniquitous, corrupt, haughty and insubordinate and insurgent children of, Israel. He bemoaned:

"Ah sinful nation,
A people laden with iniquity,
Offspring of evildoers,
Sons who deal corruptly!
They have forsaken the Lord,
They have despised the Holy One of Israel,
They are utterly estranged" (Isaiah, ch. 1).

The Lord condemned the Banú Israel for their disloyalty and for taking refuge with Pharaoh:

"Woe to the rebellious children." Says the Lord,
"Who carry out a plan, but not mine;
And who make a league, but not of my spirit,
That they may add sin to sin:
Who set out to go down to Egypt,
Without asking for my counsel,
To take refuge in the protection of the Pharoah,
And to seek shelter in the shadow of Egypt!"

(Isaiah, ch. 30).

Then came the Prophet Jeremiah who echoed the aweinspiring words of the Lord denouncing the misconduct of the Banú Israel:

"Be appalled, O heavens, at this, be shocked, be utterly desolate," says the Lord,
"For my people have committed two evils:
They have forsaken me,
The fountain of living waters,
And hewed out cisterns for themselves,
Broken cisterns, that can hold no water"

(Jeremiah, ch. 2).

Jeremiah found-the Jews of the states of Samaria and Judah to have fallen into the abyss of decrepitude, polytheism, injustice and pollution. Yet he found their "faces harder than ocks." Refusing to repent. Still did he invoke God's blessings for them. Jeremiah received a curt refusal from the Lord:

> *"How can 1 pardon you?*
> *Your children have forsaken me,*
> *And have sworn by those who are not gods"*
> *(Jeremiah, ch.* 5.).

> *"For the sons of Judah have done evil in my sight." says the Lord,*
> *"They have set their abominations in the house*
> *Which is called by my name,*
> *To defile it" (Jeremiah, ch. 7).*

Having warned the Israelites through Jeremiah, the Lord informed them that they would soon be overpowered and destroyed by "an enduring nation", coming from a far. Then does He say:

> *"And I will make to cease from the cities of Judah and from the streets of Jerusalem the voice of mirth and the voice of gladness, the voice of the bridegroom and the voice of the bride; for the land shall become waste" (Jeremiah, ch. 7).*

In the Book of Judges, the ceaseless rebels, the innovators and the disloyal among the Banú Israel seem to have provoked the Lord to anger. The Lord says:

> *"They forsook the Lord, and served Baal and Ashtaroth.*
> *So the anger of the Lord was kindled against Israel,*
> *And He gave them over to plunderers, who plundered them:*
> *And He sold them into the power of their enemies round about*
> *So that they could no longer withstand their enemies"*
> *(Judges, ch. 2.).*

The worst example of intrigue, intransigence and inhuman attitude was that set by the Jews in the case of Jesus. As he directed the missionary campaign against the strongholds of sin and slavery, the Israelites vehemently accused him of untold blasphemies. They brought him to the Roman Pilate to get him executed. Pilate entrusted the job to the half-hearted local ruler Herod, who treated the "Spirit of God" with all contempt though he failed to find anything wrong with the "accused" prophet. On receiving Jesus back, the Roman officer assembled the chief Jewish priests and the influential men and addressed them, saying:

> *"Behold, nothing deserving death has been done by him (Jesus); I will therefore chastise him and release him."*

But they all cried together:

> *"Away with this man, and release to us Barabbas—A man who had been thrown into prison for an insurrection started in the city, and for murder."*
>
> *"Pilate addressed them once more, desiring to release Jesus; but they shouted out, 'Crucify, crucify him!' " (Luke, ch. 23).*

The Holy Qur'án confirms the divine revelations to the prophets of the Banú Israel and the warnings received by them as to their iniquity and inhumanity. As to their rebellious conduct in the past, it explicitly and lucidly puts the charge-sheet against the Jews:

> *"(They have incurred divine displeasure): in that they broke their Covenant: that they rejected the Signs of God; that they slew the Messengers in defiance of right; that they said, 'Our hearts are wrappings' (which preserve God's Word; we need no more)" (4:155).*

The history of the ancient Jews could, therefore, conveniently be termed only in two simple but lawful words: *defiance* and the consequent *destruction*. From Moses and down to Jesus, the prophets and apostles of the Banú Israel had found them continually falling a prey to either of the two dangerous tendencies.

3. What the Prophet Precisely Wanted

The allegation that Muhammad was a 'persecution is untrue and groundless. On the contrary, the Prophet of Islam, wanted the Jews to do two things only: first to live with the

Muslims like trustworthy and peace-loving brothers: and, secondly (as it happened later) to accept the citizenship of the Islamic State though not the faith of Muhammad which they *prima facie* certainly undertook to fulfil the conditions of. But they did not take their pledges seriously.

4. The Invaluable Record of the Hadith

Little do the critics know about the essence of the Qur-ánic teachings, the precepts of Islam, and the literary treasures replete with the imperishable sayings of the Prophet with which they could rectify their glaring mistakes. Was it not Muhammad who had repeatedly said:

> *"Observe scrupulously the protection accorded by me to the Dhimmis (i.e., those under protection),"*
>
> *"Whoever oppresses non-Muslims (the Dhimmís), shall find me to be their advocate on the Day of Ressurrection"* (against the oppressing Muslim),"
>
> *"Remember! He who is unjust to a Dhimmís, breaks his word with him, overburdens him or dispossesses him, I shall plead against him on the Day of Judgment";*
>
> *"One who murders a Dhimmí, shall not smell of Paradise, although its fragrance can be smelt from a distance of forty years journey"; and,*
>
> *"One who persecutes a Dhimmí without a valid reason, is not from us."*

These sayings, which are couched in most humane and generous terms, have the effect and value of law with every true Muslim and Islamic society.

Obviously, therefore, it was Islam that led to the enlightenment and progress of the racially antagonistic peoples by providing them with favourable conditions to attain the same and by offering them the chances of living together as the children of Man. The magnanimity of the Prophet's treatment of other religious communities has drawn application even from the impartial non-Muslim observers.

That writes W.M. Thompson: "It is hardly too bold an assertion that to Muhammad we owe the fact that Christianity has not joined the ranks of vanished creeds."

5. Inevitability of the Punishment

The solitary instance of a justifiable punishment imposed on the Jews by Muhammad seemed inevitable. Time had come when their borrowed customs and conduct, their invocations and abominations in religious life and society, their rebellions, perfidies and disruptionist activities, were to end and they themselves were to be driven away from an area which was destined to become the Land of Bliss, and where the promised COMFORTER (as predicted by Jesus) was required to work for the resettlement of humanity without hindrance. It was there, Muhammad had to lay the foundations of a world-order that was sure to liberate man's intellect, honour and soul from the vortex of his own ambition, selfishness and criminal disposition.

Again, what happened to the Jews was perhaps to serve as a lesson to the Muslims themselves. They were, as it were, prewarned by the events that occurred then, that, if they ignored following the "light" and "guidance" brought to them by the *last Messenger,* they, too, would suffer in the manner of the strayed scriptuaries.

6. Perfidy that Brought the Punishment

Judging form the standard of upright fidelity and the necessity of living together peacefully, and from the behaviour of the Jewish clans, who were allied to the Muslims, expulsion of death was the punishment they deserved. Not only had the Jews rejected the similarities of Islam with their original faith, but they also tried to outmanoeuvre the Muslims both in peace and war. They usually added to their embarrassment when it was the question of their life and death. Thus the Qaynuqá' and the Nadhír were banished in the interests of peace, while the Qurayzah were condemned for utter disregard of the covenant that declared the Jews and the Muslims as *one people.* The death sentence passed against their warriors (with some exceptions, of course), was derived from the Law that Moses had brought to the Israelites.

7. Punishment not an Innovation

Some writers have sobbed over the "terrible" nature of the sentence given by Sa'd The Prophet had not yet received any command from his Lord to handle the cases of general perfidy. Moreover, the arbitrator himself was not unaware of the instructions in the Torah. He, accordingly, consulted the Jewish legal code in giving the award. Had the Jews trusted the Prophet himself, he might have probably sent them into exile. It would be quite appropriate to quote the *Mauláná* Muhammad 'Ali as to the nature of the sentence and the mercy that Islam preached to regulate human relations. He observes:

> "Harsh as the punishment may appear, it was exactly the judgment the Jews used to pass, under the law of their Book, against their fallen foes. Besides the heinous crime of treachery of which the Banú Qurayza were guilty, would in like circumstances be visited with no lighter punishment even in this age of civilisation. The judge was one of their own choice and the sentence was in strict conformity with their own sacred law. Again, they were guilty of treachery of a dangerous nature. Is there any sense in finding fault with the Prophet on this account? The objection against the harshness of this punishment is an objection against the Mosaic Law. It is, in fact, an unconscious censure of that Law as well as an admission that a more humane law must come to supersede it. A contrast with the Islamic law on this point will bring out into clear relief what tender, sympathetic and compassionate law Islam came to inaugurate."

8. The Prophet as Pledge

The Jews did not respect their pledges, but the Prophet of Islam was always very particular in their observance. Minding least what the other party would do with their promises. Muhammad took his undertaking quite seriously. For instance, at the time of the battle of Uhud, he discovered that a certain number of Jews from Medina who had joined his army had asked to go back; for they said they had no obligation in respect of the defence of Medina that involved fighting outside the town.

9. The Jews Prevent Truth from Reaching the Needy

Another fault of the Jews in the Prophet's time was that they always engaged themselves in causing disruption in the Muslim society. Besides rejecting the truth themselves, they dissuaded others from accepting it readily. While commenting on this point 'Abdulláh Yúsuf 'Ali writes:

> "There are many ways of preventing the access of people to the truth. One is to tamper with it, or trick it out in colours of falsehood. Another is to conceal it altogether. Those who are jealous of a man of God, whom they actually see before them, do not allow his credentials or virtues to be known, or vilify him, or conceal facts which would attract people to him. When people do this of set purpose against their own light ('of which ye are yourselves witnesses'), they are descending to the lowest depths of degradation, and they are doing more harm to themselves than to anyone else."

10. An Arab Prophet Unacceptable to the Jews

One of the chief causes of the trouble with the Jews was, that while they expected the appearance of a prophet or Messiah, Muhammad was not acceptable to them. The Judaic community did not consider a non-Israelite fit for the divine office. They rejected the very idea that an Arab could be deputed with an exalted mission of the prophethood. It was an enigma to them that a backward people or the "Gentiles" should produce a Messenger of God. This kind of thinking was due to the complex from which the Jews had suffered throughout their history.

11. Comparing Kinds of Treatment of the Vanquished

In comparison with what the conqueror did with the defeated, the Prophet's attitude toward the Jews was distinctly better and more befitting. It was a practice with him that he would not permit his emotions and the emotions of his followers to come in his way while settling matters with the vanquished parties, be they the Jews, the Bedouins or the Quraysh. As against this, let us see how the victors have from time to time treated their losing foes. The destruction of the Jewish culture and towns and the enslavement of the Jews, first under the Babylonians and then under Vespasian, may be kept in view, in 70 C.E., Vespasian's son captured Jerusalem, killed 137,000 took 67,000 captive, besides sending thousands of the Jews to the Egyptian mines for forced labour and deporting others to the alien cities to be used for hunts and by the hunters and in the theatres. The tall and beautiful females of the Jews were chosen for company by the Romans.

In modern times, the winners of the trophy of war, never pardoned the defeated nations as did Muhammad in the sixth century. For instance, when World War One terminated, the peace that Germany was asked to sign, was so humiliating that none among the Germans volunteered to put his signatures on the draft treaty. It was considered a slur on their national honour to do so. And those who ultimately went to negotiate the terms were treated as worse than prisoners. As to the contents of the peace itself, they were too unrealistic and heavy to be borne by the German nation. The indemnity imposed on Germany was unimaginable. Her whole mercantile marine was captured by the victors. She was deprived of all her territories outside Europe, besides minerally rich Alsace and Loraine. Her military strength was reduced to nothingness. In a word, the Germans lay prostrate before the retaliating conquerors.

12. Comparing "Injustices", Alleged or Otherwise

Whatever the nature and magnitude of an act of "persecution" and extermination of a community, it may not diminish the gravity of a crime. While judging an action in the light of compelling factors (as in the case of the Prophet of Islam), it should be estimated along with the real instances of gross injustice done to rightful peoples who offended no one and who were bound by no agreements with any party. In the present-day world, the Muslim communities have become targets of repression and oppression at the hands of those who have come to possess resources and grab power. Their very birthright is being violated. We may cite the example of the Palestinians who were driven out in order to set up a "national home" for the *lost sheep* of Israel, who were ever accustomed to demanding miracles and the manna dew from their prophets. The bringing together of heterogeneous elements persecuted elsewhere, amounts to a crime that posterity will never forgive; for is it not unimaginable that the Jewish families, spread all over the world, should have been regarded to be within their rights to erect a "home" for themselves on the heads of the original dwellers? These and the Zionists, who could be compared to a mastless vessel, blasted into fragments by the cyclones of the time, were huddled together like the broken parts of that vessel from the vast ocean of history, "rebuilt" through international artifices and then offered anchorage on the eastern shores of the Mediterranean against the will of all the Palestinians—whether they were Muslims, true Jews or sincere Christians, not to speak of the Islamic world at large.

Which of the two "injustices" and "punishments" is greater, ask the sensitive well-wishers of humanity? Is it Muhammad's or that of the Zionists and their supporters? There is no justification for the latter; for is it not a fact that the rulers had recognised the Jews as a community having historical links with Jerusalem? Had the Palestinian Jews not been assured for all their political and civil rights? Why were then the Arabs—the owners of land with permanent interests at stake—brutally turned out and hunted down? Why were their hearths extinguished for no fault of theirs? An impartial observer would prefer to bracket the Zionists of this century with the ancient Babylonians the Assyrians, the Greco-Romans, and emperor Vespasian (or Titus), all of whom had invariably subjugated the Jews, brushed aside their homes, made them captive, suppressed their culture and laid their cities and temples waste. The Prophet Muhammad did not leave a legacy to that effect, but had enjoined tolerance. Is it not, therefore, unwarrantable that the critics should blame him and now even go so far as to justify the act of dispossessing his followers?

13. Past Favours *vs.* Brute Force of the Present

Finally, some of the points in the article of Nissim Rejwan necessitate elucidation. First, the contributor admits that at times "certain historical truths are in more need of re-examination than others." The present writer's endeavour, in the first part of this essay has been to present a "consistent" and "unprejudiced re-statement" of the respective positions of the Jews and the Muslims in Arabia. The writer sincerely hopes that such a re-statement will help reduce the prevailing tension and animosity. But what of the consequences of the Palestine Partition Plan of 1947 C.E., which was imposed from outside and of which the destructive and unholy traces will continue to threaten peace until justice is done to the Arab refugees, about two million of whom are ceaselessly knocking at the doors of the war-mongers and the torchbearers of peace, both having once combined to have them unsettled within a year?

Secondly, the remark of the Jewish contributor, that as against the Arab States, the Jewish society treats its "Arab members" with "reserve", is more than surprising. It may be said in answer to this that if it did not maintain reserved the Zionist society would be implementing completely the sentence of injustice against the wronged Arabs. Moreover. It is for its own preservation and for finding time to digest what Zionism has devoured in the past two decades that the quality of reserve must continue. Also, it would help avoid the general resentment of the Muslims all over the globe.

Thirdly, the article *Judeo-Arabic Civilisation,* shows that the Jewish *litterateurs* have come to recognize the fact that

Islam carried with it blessing for the Jewish race thus "wherever the Crescent bore rule, the lot of the Jews again to improve" in Palestine, Egypt. Iraq. Syria and Spain In the last mentioned country, the Muslims brought to the Jews not only relief from their oppressions but, in the words of Dr. Isidore Epstein (a Jew). "Also encouraged among them culture which in richness and depth is comparable to the best produced by any people at any time." In his book, *Judism and Islam,* Dr. Erwin Rosenthal, of Cambridge, has received that, "the Talmudic Age apart, there is perhaps no more formative and positive period in our long and chequered history than that under the empire of Islam from the Mediterranean to the Indian Ocean." The Arabs, it is said, "turned Spain into by far the most enlightened country in Europe." The Jews shared this enlightenment unhindered. They acquired progress and prosperity everywhere under Islamic rule, because their Muslim brethren were devoted to the arts of peace.

Of this be the historical truth, is it not correct to say, as Professor Arnold J. Toynbee more than once stated, that the worst sin committed against the Arabs was to make them homeless by creating a Zionist "state"? This meant installing an entity which was manufactured from beyond the Arab lands. In the end, the present writer would like to pose a question to the scholars and statesmen who have had a "grand role" to play in squeezing a homeland out of the confused and scattered imagination of the Jews: could there be no other solution to the Jewish problem, born of European tyranny, than tyrannizing instead the innocent Arabs and raising a new problem by obliging them to become the unfortunate substitutes for the tyrannised Jews? The writer believes that they owe an answer to the lovers of humanity, to posterity and to the younger generations of the Islamic Community.

[***By:*** *—Dr. Sheikh Muhammad Iqbal*
Source: *The Islamic Review & Arab Affairs,*
June 1970.]

9

Prayer and its Importance to Individuals & Nations

Its Meaning, Its Reality, Its Power

An Acceptable Definition of Prayer

Prayer has been defined as "the act by which man, conscious at once of his weakness and of his immortality, puts himself into real and effective communication with the Almighty, the Eternal, the self-Existent God."

This is not a definition of prayer which could be universally applied. People have been known to pray who never believed in their own immortality or in an Eternal and self Existent God. Even to this day masses of people can be seen in India going to their idols with rice and flowers to offer prayers and supplications for the recovery of their beloved child or their pet cow.

It is true that prayer is generally the result of the consciousness of man of his own weakness, and so also of the superiority or strength of the other person or being to whom prayer is offered, either directly or through a medium.

It is true that the evolved consciousness of men does not stoop to pray except to a living, almighty omniscent, and omnipresent Deity; for an advanced humanity the realm of human power and might has been greatly extended even beyond the imagination of human beings of remote ages. How can a man with knowledge and sense now pray to a tree or stone? How can he even pray to the sun or the moon, when he has become conscious of the fact that he has in him certain capacities which make him master of the tree and stone, the sun and moon? The sun and moon, the tree and stone, have no will of their own. Man has, and so man is superior to them. If we limit prayer to its modern meaning, we can use the definition given above with a little more particularization—perhaps something like this:

Prayer is an act by which humanity, conscious at once of its physical weakness and inner strength, puts itself, either directly or indirectly, into real and effective communication with the Almighty, the Living, the Omniscent, and the Omnipresent God. Who responds to human call.

Prayers to God who is not almighty and omnipresent, prayers to a "finite person", cannot carry much conviction, and their efficacy is also marred. If our God has no power or is not willing to help us in all difficulties, anywhere and any time, then there is not much use calling upon Him.

Prayer brings man into real and effective communication with God, so prayer is the medium through which man imbibes the attributes of his Maker—His all-comprehensive, impartial, inexhaustive beneficence. His mercy, even His majesty and might. Prayer is the key to piety.

The Qur'án on the conception of piety

But piety does not consist in merely going to church on one day—it does not consist in repeating fixed formula of any particular religion. Prayers, mere lip-prayers, without the co-operation of the heart, without the co-operation of our whole being, are meaningless—they can do no good. By mere lip-prayers we do not imbibe the attributes of God. They do good neither to us nor to the world. It is only real prayers, real piety, which do good to individuals and nations and the world at large.

> *There is no piety in turning your face towards the East and the West (in your formal prayers), but he is pious (he is prayerful) who believes in God and the Day of Judgment, the angels, the*

> *scriptures, and the prophets who for the love of God (i.e., not with selfishness) disburses his wealth to his kindred, and to the orphans, and the needy and the wayfarer, and to those who ask for, and for the redemption of a captive who observes prayer and gives alms, and who is of those who are faithful of their engagements when they have covenanted, and who are patient in adversity, and hardship and in times of trouble. These are they who are straight, these are they who are pious* (The Qur'án, 2:177).

These are they who have themselves profited by their prayers, and who have added to the progress of this world by their sympathy with and help for their fellow-men.

Prayer is an outpouring of its love and gratitude by the human soul to its Maker, to its Cherisher. Prayer is an expression of human desire for the help and guidance of the Master, whatever name may be given to Him. Prayer is an expression of the craving of the human soul to be in communion with Him from Whom it came. The reality of prayer consists in its coming out of the human soul to Him Who is the origin and the real essence of the human soul its reality consists in its being natural, in its linking the soul to its essence and also in its communicating to man his dependence upon the mercy and love of God, or Allah, Brahma, or Jehovah.

A Thoughtful Person Should be More Prayerful

When a man comes in this world what does he find? He finds that all arrangements for his existence had already been made before he came in the world. There is pure air to breathe, and there are also other natural necessities for his existence. There is the wonderfully nutritious milk to drink. Besides, in the maternal mind special affection and love have already been placed for him which look not only to his necessities, but also to his luxuries. As a baby he is absolutely helpless. At that time of his life he cannot defend himself. But means have been provided which make him—a helpless baby though he is, a defenceless little mite though he is—flourish and grow up into manhood. He, when he grows up, might prove himself a rouge and a villain, he, when he grows up, might one day be seen on the gallows, but when he is a baby such wonderful arrangements have been made that he finds himself among people—at least two such people—that would sooner give up their own life than see any harm coming to him. What would a mother not do to see her child happy and well!

Who provided all those natural requirements for his existence? Who put such a love and affection in the heart of his mother and of his father that they nourished him and spent money over his bringing up, even at personal sacrifices? Surely, he himself did not do it. Then, should he not be grateful for all that was provided for him, for all that was done for him? Should he not be prayerful to Him who was so merciful and compassionate as to provide everything which he was expected to require for his existence?

The great S'adí of Shíráz (d. 1292 C.E.), a Persian poet, has said that man should be prayerful and thankful to God twice at every breath. First, because when he breathes out he sends out the air which was obnoxious to his health, and this saves his life; secondly, because when he breathes in he inhales life-giving oxygen.

An advanced man who does some scientific research work should be more conscious of these hidden bounties of God which were waiting to be discovered to help in the advancement of human comfort and civilization. If these hidden forests for coal and oil had not been provided for, ages ago, by a providential nature in anticipation of the invention of the steam-engine, the internal combustion engine, half the material progress of the world would be impossible today. Should not man then be thankful for all that has been provided for him, even in anticipation of his needs and progress?

There can be no doubt that man owes a great deal, in fact all, to a merciful providence, and so a prayer to Him cannot but be real an instinctive expression of human gratefulness. The sense of weakness of common to whole humanity, therefore is the instinct of prayer common.

The more man realizes his dependence on the mercy and will of God as a higher Being, the more his prayers will be real and sincere. Even the cleverest scientist of the age cannot deny that human life can be destroyed in a second by accidents. The fact is that there is nothing strange in death. It is the life which is a marvel. Think of all those poisonous germs which co-exist with man in this world. Think of all those accidents which can occur to any man any minute. And then will it be possible to realize human dependence upon Providence, and then will the reality of prayer be impressed upon the human mind. The love a child has for its mother is real, so is the hankering of the human soul for its Author, its parent, its original. The more a man realizes his true position in the scheme of things of the world, the more man becomes conscious of the immortality of his soul, of his inner strength, of his true origin, of the *raison d'être* of his existence, the more real his prayers are.

THE REALITY OF PRAYERS IS ALSO THE POWER OF PRAYER

The Human Soul and Its Relationship With God, its Creator

The human soul is not mortal.

"Dust thou art, to dust returnest,
Was not spoken of the Soul."

The Qur'án, 38:72, says, "*Nafakhtu fi-hi min rúhi*" (I, God, breathed My Soul into man).

Jesus said, "Believest thou not that I am in the Father and the Father in me? The words that I speak unto you I speak not of myself, but the Father that dwelleth in me He doeth the works" (John xiv. 10). The sayings of great Hindu saints are full of such sentiments.

A great Muslim saint has also said:

"I became Thou and Thou becamest me. I became the body and Thou the Soul.

"So that nobody should say any more that I am different and Thou art different."

Not only have the three sister religions—Judaism, Christianity and Islam—taught man to believe that he possesses something of Divine in him, but so did even the old religions. He is weaker than many animals. At a certain time of his life he is more helpless even than an ant. An ant can find its food, but a human baby at its birth cannot even do that. Physically, man is a weak creature. He has not developed much more than his "ancestor", the ape, in certain physical respects.

God is Infinite. God is free from all weakness. God has no physicality. When man puts himself in "real and effective communication" with God, he does so only through his spirit. And because God is All-powerful—Almighty—this spiritual communication with Him, which man secures through prayer, gives him power and might. It is not easy to explain exactly spiritual affairs by words spoken by mouth or written by pen, and it is not easy to explain how prayer gives power. But some idea can be formed if we, for the sake of illustration, and illustration only, take God to be a centre of electricity. When we pray we connect, as it were, a wire to that centre and get a current off that electricity. The stronger the wire—that is, the more sincere, solemn and pure our prayers are—the more strength we shall get. Through the power thus gained men have performed wonderful miracles. When man submits his own will to the will of God, when man gets into communion with his Maker, he can do many more things than "are dreamt of in philosophy." The maxim "Thy will and not mine", if fully acted upon, can make man do wonders. It can awaken all that is Divine in man.

The human soul holds the first rank among all created things, because it has something of Divine in it. It is immortal because it has something of Divine in it. Its power is also due to the same reason. It is the human soul which should rule the body if man desires to be above animals. Man's duty as man, as being higher to all other creation, higher even than the sun and the moon, is to cultivate his soul, to cultivate and develop in him that part which is Divine. If he does so he will become powerful. He will be able not only to rule his own body, but also that of others. His eyesight will become clearer; he will be able to see the departed souls, will be able to talk to them. The future will be as clear to him as the present. He will be able to read the very thoughts of the living persons. He will be able to transfer his thoughts, without any physical or material medium, thousands of miles. By his will he will be able to influence and even dominate the wills of others. He will be able to rule even over the elements. Knowledge is power. What is knowledge? A development of the latent faculties in man to enquire into and grasp the realties of things. Knowledge depends upon reason, and reason is but one of the many functions of the soul. By the development of reason and wisdom alone man has been able to master the air and the sea. How much more power could he get if he would develop the soul fully and perfectly? The perfection of the soul is only possible by linking it with it Original—from whom it came and to whom it returneth. What is that link? Prayer. By a real and effective communication with God we can secure power. Hence, man has been advised to seek assistance from patience and prayer in the time of affliction and trouble. *Ista'ínú bi al-Sabr wa al-Saláh* (seek help with patience and prayer—The Qur'án 2:153).

Prayer Gives Power to Those Who Pray

By prayer one can approach the Almighty. By approaching the Almighty one can secure power. Thus, by prayer one can secure power. Prayer is the manifestation of human weakness as compared with the Almighty power that rules over him and the whole universe. But it is also a means of securing such power as to enable man to become the vicegerent of that Almighty God Himself, and to rule over all other creatures. Because prayer gives man a knowledge of his own weakness, and because knowledge is power, therefore, even as a manifestation of weakness, prayer is in truth nothing but power. When a man has purified his soul, when he has put himself in effective communication with God through prayer, his power extends over the dead and the living, over the organic and inorganic parts of the world. He can never be God. He can never be all-powerful. Even at his best he can have but an infinitesimal current from that *Centre of Electricty.* But his spiritual power can, through that electric current, infinitesimal though it be, transcend not only his physical strength, but that of all other creatures. He can rule all other creatures which do not posses that current even to the extent he possesses. He can continue to develop that power more and ever more. Physical death cannot stop him from that development. Prayer can give power not only when man is in his physical body, but also when he leaves for regions higher and heavenly. It is, therefore, that those who are in Paradise are always engaged in prayer—i.e. in more and more purification of the soul, in greater and greater progress and advance. They secure greater and yet greater power.

THE PLACE AND VALUE OF PRAYER TO THE INDIVIDUAL

Prayer is a pillar of faith. It is the diet of the human soul. The human soul cannot rest content unless and until it has held communion with its Origin. Everything delights when it is in its own elements, so does the soul. The soul is in its elements when it is in communion with God. The best way to hold communion with God is prayer.

Prayer has the same effect on our souls as protoplasm has on our physical bodies. Prayer supplies nourishment for the soul, and it is for this reason that certain religions, like Islam, have made even formal prayer obligatory five times a day. Physical body seeks nourishment five times a day, so does the human soul. In fact, the human soul should be more looked after than the human body. Human body is mortal: it decays; even if it is looked after with all possible care it cannot last long. It can never be made immortal. All the pleasure and pain it gives, or gets, can but be transitory. But human soul is immortal. The more nourished it is, the more happiness it will give, and as its happiness shall be everlasting, it deserves to be more valued. Man must look to his spiritual good even more than to his physical good. In any case, he must not neglect his soul. If he does not hold his communion with God, if he does not pray to his God, he is sure to neglect his soul. He must not live by bread alone, but by the words of mouth—by prayer, as Jesus Christ has instructed: his prayers must find a place in his daily life. The prayer of the heart needs no language. The well-known Persian mystic Háfiz (d. 1388 C.E.) says:

"Relate thou the incidents of love in whatever language thou knowest."

And Hakím Siná'í (d. 1150 C.E.) another Persian poet says:

"When thou speakest of Faith speak it in any language thou knowest, whether it be Hebraic or Syrian:

"When thou seekest the abode of Truth seek it in and country, whether Jábalqa or Jábalsá."

Prayer may be offered without the use of a single word, but offered it must be. Human nature demands it, craves for it. Very often man becomes prayerful instinctively. In distress and in danger, particularly on board a ship, in mid-ocean, when a storm rages, even such men have been found to have taken recourse to prayer that never did so before. Even such persons that did not believe in God became believers when overtaken by some serious afflction. It is, as it were, instinctive to look to God for help when man finds himself in trouble. And what a solace, what a comfort, a sincere prayer affords to the human mind when every other means to secure comfort and satisfaction is found wanting! Prayer affords a great spiritual and moral satisfaction to a believing mind. It saves man from despondency and despair. It encourages him to face danger and even death. It induces him to work even when he finds his work hard. He feels more active. His prayer has an energizing effect on him. He knows that everything in this world depends upon a cause; that for every work exertion is necessary. But then, experiment teaches him that no man in the world, as yet, has been able to master all circumstances.

Even with the best human effort the cherished object is sometimes not achieved because of some sudden adverse circumstance. Sometimes it requires repeated efforts to secure success. Sometimes it is after repeated failures that success is gained. He may do his best and work his utmost to secure the means of his success, but how can he master all unforeseen circumstances? He is not the master of the world. He cannot foresee every possible incident. He cannot forfend even possible accident. But he knows that God is master of all that exists. He knows that by securing His help he can avoid all adverse circumstances over which he himself has no control. While he does his best, all that is humanly possible to achieve his object, he instinctively feels that he must also avoid all adverse circumstances and accidents, and must approach by solemn and sincere prayers Him who is Almighty and All-powerful to vouchsafe him His help. Because God says in the Qur'án, 40:60 "Pray unto Me and I shall answer", a man feels doubly confident of success when he mingles his prayers to his God with his own efforts to achieve his object. The more confident we are of success, the more hard work we can put in. By prayer we get more confident: therefore, if we are prayerful we can put in more work and more enthusiasm.

Because prayer saves from despair, being addressed to Him who is All-powerful, who is above all laws and circumstances, it encourages a man to face failure after failure. Human endeavours might fail. But if prayer secures God's assistance failure becomes impossible. Why then should he despair? Why should he not make another effort with a whole-hearted prayer even if he has failed once, twice, or a hundred times? If he has faith in prayer, failure will never tire him out.

The Moral Value of Prayer to the Individual

The moral value of prayer to the individual is also very high. God is perfect. He is all-holy. When a man seeks communion with Him through prayer, he has to see that he does not approach Him with an unholy heart, with an impure mind. It is for this reason that it has been said:

> *"Rehearse that which has been revealed to you of the Book, and be constant at prayer, for prayer preserves from crimes and from that which is blameable; and the remembering of God is surely a most sacred duty"* (The Qur'án, 29:45).

With a guilty conscience, nobody can have a heart to go to Him who is all-knowing, all-holy and pure, and who is omnipresent. The good of instituting repeated formal prayers every day is the same. That helps to awaken man's conscience. When he goes to pray he has to present himself before God. He has to judge himself and his doings every time he goes to prayer to be judged by his God, and this quite naturally has a beneficent moral effect upon him.

As regards the spiritual place and value of prayer, prayer has the first and foremost place and the highest value. It is only by repeated communication and communion with God that we can purify our soul, our spirit, and we must make ourselves fit for communion with God.

Prayer is valuable to the individual, to man, because it discovers himself to him—it reveals to man his weakness and also his greatness, what is mortal in him and what is immortal in him. *Nosceteipsum*[1] is a good motto. Shakespeare has truly said that he who is true to himself will consequently be true to others. And still a grander saying is, "He who knows himself knows his Lord." Through prayer man knows himself; through prayer man knows his Lord.

An iron when it is put in the fire takes in many attributes of fire. In the same way does wood also; but while the wood gets burnt quickly to ashes, the iron does not. A human soul also in communion with God takes in God's attributes. If, however, the soul is not prepared and purified beforehand, it will not be like iron but rather like wood. Moral purity, in certain respects even physical purity, is concomitant with spiritual purity. When a man possessing physical, moral and spiritual purity engages in prayer, his soul with God is like iron with fire. Thus, morally and spiritually both, prayer should hold a high place in individual life. Its value is great in moulding the character of the individual, in saving him from despair and in giving him encouragement in his work.

What Kind of Prayer Finds Acceptance With God?

A prayer with good motives, with sincere desire, and one which has the good either of the individual or community as its objective, is sure to be heard. But even if it is not heard for the time being it is not in vain. It does one good simply to pray. It is a moral gain to the individual. It is his duty to pray. Háfiz sweetly says:

> *"Hafiz wazífah'e tú dú á guftanast o bas*
> *Dar band án mabash kih nashuníd yá shuníd."*

(O Háfiz, it is thy duty to pray and nothing else.
Take no thought whether He hears thee or not).

In Isaiah I, 14-17, is given these conditions which make the prayers acceptable:

> *"Your new moons and your appointed feasts my soul hateth: they are a trouble unto me: I am weary to bear them. And when ye spread forth your hands, I will hide mine eyes from you: yea, when ye make many prayers, I will not hear: your hands are full of blood. Wash you, make you clean: put away the evil of your doings from before mine eyes; cease to do evil; learn to do well: seek judgment, relieve the oppressed, judge the fatherless, plead for the widow."*

A man has a right to go to his Creator and Cherisher for everything—even for temporal benefits, for his daily bread, for rain, etc. however low the object of the prayer be, the very fact that the man has gone to his God for it is a moral gain. It matters not if different persons pray to the same Deity, at the same time, for contrary things. It is not man's business to anticipate the difficulties in the way of the prayer being heard. Nothing is impossible for God, and He knows best which prayer should be heard and which rejected. He has ordained that all that is humanly possible to achieve an object, however temporal should be done by man, and for the success of the undertaking sincere prayer should be offered and the help of Him invoked who is the Master of the Universe.

The greatest work which was set to Moses by the all Wise God was to uplift a down-trodden nation. That nation was morally degraded, therefore, it was politically in bondage. If

Moses had united the spiritual regeneration of the nation with its moral and physical regeneration, that would have been too much for its capacities; therefore, for the time being, he contented himself with leading his people out of bondage and with improving their morals through rigid laws and strict discipline. He had to be firm and rigid in his laws, and he was perhaps a little too firm and rigid in making his people work for their liberty. The development of the ideas of after-life and of prayer was left to later prophets and reformers.

Almost All Religions Recognise the Institution of Prayer

Almost every religious *system* worth the name has recognized the institution of prayer. That is, every church has found prayer to be of some value: The early Hindu temples were crowded with men with their offerings and sacrifices. Invocations and *Mantrás,* or prayers, were also repeated. The *Bhagwat Gitá* is a spiritual and energizing book of great value to the Hindu Church up to this day. But among Hindus the existence of a priestly class—the Brahmans—deprived, as it were, the masses of their individual right of worship and prayer. It was only through the Brahmans that any worship, any prayer, could be conducted. Perhaps it strengthened the position of the Hindu Church in a way, but sacrifice and prayer lost nearly all their moral and spiritual value. Modern tendency of Hindus is to curtail the power of priests.

The Zoroastrians were a very prayeful people. So were the Magians. But with these also spiritual life became the monopoly of the ministers of religion. Among the great religious systems. Buddhism has been unique in respect of its ideas of God Himself, and also its ideas about prayers to Him. Buddhism has no church. It has dispensed with prayer, or rather has substituted meditation for prayer, although there is not very much difference between the two.

The credit that is Jesus's

The credit of expounding noble ideas of our future life and of giving the true character to prayer rests with Jesus. It is true that the Jews, shortly after the Great Law-giver Moses, also became prayerful people. The idea of God became less anthropomorphized, and from the primitive use of the name of Jehovah in invocation regular and serious prayer developed; but it was through Jesus Christ that prayer realized its spiritual height. The value of prayer to the Christian Church is immeasurable. There is no religion in the world which has such a highly organized Church system as Christianity. And the Church owes its organization mostly to prayer. Missals, councils, liturgies, and convocations were held to settle articles of faith, and matters of conscience. The Lord's day institution has been of the greatest possible value to the Church. As the Lord's Prayer is a glorious prayer, so from the Church point of view is the Lord's day a glorious day; a day reserved for prayer and worship is a very beneficent institution for the Church. In these days of skepticism, but for Sunday institution as a day of prayer, there would hardly have been any prayer in congregation, and the Church system would have suffered greatly. Congregational prayers which are said under the auspices of the Church are more acceptable to God, even though the congregation be very small.

> *And again I say unto you, that is two of you shall agree on earth as touching anything that they shall ask, it shall be done for them of my Father which is in heaven. For where two or three are gathered together in my name, there am I in the midst of them* (Matthew xix. 20).

Intercession, Holy Communion, mediator's prayer, prayer of consecration, confession, etc., all played important parts in increasing the value of prayer for the Church of Christianity. Congregational prayers under the Church give the Church a hold over the conscience of the nation. In fact, the Church rules the masses through prayer. Of course for the purpose of the Church some formalism had to be given to the prayers, and prayer lost its voluntary effect. Not only man but everything created by God should know its prayer to its Creator. Every individual should have the amplest scope for the heartiest outpouring of love and gratitude devotion and humility to his Maker. Cherisher and Sustainer—to the all-merciful and compassionate yet requiting and reckoning God. Islam is the religion which, while establishing formal and congregational prayers as well, has seen to it most of all other religions that the value of prayers be not lost to the individual. Islam is too democratic in its character to have allowed any Church organization to have been perfected in it. It has no priests, and no church can exist without priests. Besides this, as an English writer. Mr. Hunter, says: "It is one of the glories of Islam that its temples are not made with hands, and that its ceremonies can be performed anywhere upon God's earth or under His heaven."

Still, Islam has established formal congregational prayers. There are prayers said five times a day, which should preferably be said in congregation and in a Mosque. There is also an institution of Friday prayers in congregation said in Mosques. There are other large congregational prayers of 'Id said twice a year. But the value of these prayers is more to the State and nation than to the Church of Islam. Every Muslim has his church in him. Any Muslim can lead the prayers. Any Muslim can say formal prayers for his dead brother. Any Muslim can bind two willing persons in marriage anywhere. It is, therefore, that the church system in Islam is not so well organized as it is in Christianity and it is, therefore, that there is no church to which prayers so valuable as it is to the Christian Church. In fact nearly all formal prayers, except the Lord's Prayer, of Christianity have been the work of the Church. It will not be wrong to say that to the Christian prayers the Church has been as valuable as the prayers to the Church. In Islam all formal prayers are to be the same as those which were said by Muhammad himself. However, generally speaking, prayers are the backbone of the Church—every church.

THE VALUE OF PRAYER TO THE STATE

The value of prayer to the State in Christian and Buddhistic countries is getting less and less, because there religion itself has been divorced from the State. In England that schism is not so great as in other Christian countries. In England there is a State church, although that Church has given up even the moral and social care of the people to the State. The State can reach the heart of the people through the Church, and as the church has to use the medium of prayer to reach the masses, the value of prayer becomes great to the State. The greater the value of prayers as a moral agent, the more their value to the State. A man who is true to God cannot but be true to himself and to his fellow-creatures. The State is always in need of such men.

On such emergencies and catastrophes as great wars, the value of congregational prayers to the State becomes very great indeed, because it is through prayer that the State can make an appeal to the public to make a solemn, united and hearty effort to achieve peace and victory. The State secures the moral support of the whole nation through organized prayers. The State secures the will of the whole nation to win the war through prayers.

Since prayers are always more sincere at the time of distress and affliction, and they appeal most to a merciful God, the State gets a spiritual support also through prayers at a time of national crisis.

There is one more gain secured to the State through prayers, and it is that when the life of a number of near and dear relations of the people is at stake they are more in a prayerful mood to secure, as it were, the safety of their relations. But when they go to pray the idea naturally comes to them that they should not expect their prayers to be answered unless they are offered with a chaste mind, and then they try to free themselves of impurities. This gives to the State better citizens to deal with. France found it to its cost during the First Great War that it was not quite the right policy for the State to have ignored the Church. There was a revival of religiousness in France. The churches were not quite neglected and the attendance for prayer in the churches was not small. The State also benefited by the Red Cross organization.

Generally speaking, however, the value of prayers to Muslim State is the highest, and so is the value of prayer to the Muslim nation. Muslim congregational prayers breathe the spirit of democracy, equality and fraternity, and as they are held every day a number of times, they have a wholesome and lasting effect on the mind of the people. Muslim formal prayers are also good for the State and the nation, because they teach every day lessons in early rising, punctuality and cleanliness to the people. They have very high moral value and have great disciplinary effects. They teach humility before God, before whom every Muslim prostrates in his prayers, and have a beneficent influence on the devotee's general character when he finds himself in the presence of the Omniscient and Omnipresent God five times every day. This repeated presence before the Great Judge does great good to the individual, and as it is the individuals who form the nations and States, the value of prayer to the nation and State is not less than to the individual. Prayer teaches man to do his duty. The State demands the same. The State cannot work unless its citizens are taught to do their duty. Thus, prayers are very helpful to the State.

THE VALUE OF PRAYER IN EVERYDAY AFFAIRS OF LIFE, IN HEALING AND IN SICKNESS

It has been said that the institution of one day as the day of prayer has helped in the organization of the Church. But it must also be acknowledged that it has not been such a beneficial institution to the individual for his everyday life. It has, in a way, given an encouragement to the people to reserve only one day for prayers and the rest of the week for the business of the world. This has, as it were, made the care of the soul less important than that of the body. Human affairs of ordinary life should be conducted with purity of mind. Prayer is the best agent to secure purity of mind. Prayers, formal prayers, congregational prayers, should be said every day to keep the mind in a pure condition. He who fears God has to fear nothing else. If a man finds himself fit to approach the all-knowing God a number of times every day, he will face any work without fear. And how very valuable a prayer like the following is to lighten our daily work to us:

> *O Lord! Punish us not if we forget, or fall into error. O our Lord! lay not on us a load like that which Thou hast laid on those which were before us. O our Lord! and lay not on us that for which were have not strength* (The Qur'án, 2:286).

All men can say to their God, "Show us the right path", in every walk of life, in every work they have to undertake.

Our daily work should begin with prayers. Prayers should influence our daily life. The value of prayer increases immensely if we do not separate our daily work from our prayers. It is not right to let rest and worship go together—to reserve only one day for prayer as well as rest. Rather work and prayer should go together. Our prayers should sanctify our work and bless it. We should always be ready to attend to the call to prayer. We should always be willing to sacrifice our daily comfort, even our worldly work, to attend to the needs of our soul. There is no doubt that as long as we live in this world we must not neglect our work. But we must not neglect our soul either. If work is necessary to get bread and bread necessary for sustenance of the body, so is prayer necessary for the sustenance of the soul. Therefore, work and prayer should both take a part in our everyday life. Prayers keep our minds clean, our life clean, and our work clean. They save us from going wrong—in speech, in act, even in thought.

Prayer cannot but have a healing and curing effect if it really puts the devotee in an effective and real communication with the all-Beneficent, Merciful and Powerful God. It has been experienced by many physicians that the willpower of the patient and the innate vitality of the spirits play an important part in bringing the disorganized system of the human body to its normal condition. Prayer, if it is sincere, if it really means an application to the all-Beneficent God, must be a source of strength to the willpower and must have a reviving effect on the spirits. The firmer the faith of a person in God, the greater the influence or prayer on his spirits, and through his spirits also on his physical body. People quite healthy in body have sometimes died by sudden excitement of pain or pleasure. Cheerful news sometimes does more to uplift the spirits of man than a dose of strong tonic. Prayer can take the place of cheerful news. It can arouse the drooping spirits. It can produce health-giving excitement. It was by empirical knowledge that man first found out that such and such herb is useful for such and such an ailment. It was by experience that it was found out that prayers are helpful in reviving the spirits of persons who are religiously inclined. It is not only healing and curing that man can do through prayers, but many more things, provided that the prayer really becomes a means of communion with God. it is revelation from God Himself which teaches man how his prayers can become a means of communion with God. Hence the necessity for Divine messengers to teach man effective prayers. But in this material world of ours it will not be right to expect that prayers alone will join a broken leg. Man has been given wisdom and reason to find out medicines for his physical ailments, and he must use that wisdom and reason and find out medicine for any disease of his body. God in His mercy provided medicines for all ailments of the body. But man is weak. His knowledge is also imperfect. Prayer should be used to make up for the human weakness by securing the help of the Almighty God. Prayer should be used to make up for the deficiency of human knowledge, for guidance in the diagnosis of the ailment and the right use of the proper medicine.

THE VALUE OF PRAYER IN TIMES OF DISTRESS AND NATIONAL DANGER AND IN RELATION TO A NATIONAL IDEAL AND WORLD PROGRESS

The value of prayer in times of distress and national danger has been discussed before. The greater the danger to the nation, the more necessary it becomes to secure a united effort, not only physical but also moral and spiritual, on the part of the whole nation to meet that danger. Moral and spiritual, and through that physical effort could best be secured by common prayer which will bring home to every heart the danger that the nation has to face, and would impress upon the whole people their community of interest. In an organized State any desire of the nation, if it is expressed unanimously, finds a ready response. To the King of all kings a unanimous petition sent in the form of hearty prayers cannot remain unanswered. The moral and spiritual effect of prayers at the time of distress and national danger is very great. The material effect is also not small, because it unites the whole people on one point, and union is always strength. Prayer also encourages in the individual the spirit of mutual help, sacrifice and self-abnegation, and at a time of national danger the spirit of mutual help and sacrifice in the individuals cannot but be most valuable to the nation and to the State.

Prayer also sets national ideals. For example: what was the national ideal the Muslim nation in its early rise set before it? The same which has found expression in its prayer: "O Lord! Thou art our Maker. Give us success against the idolatrous people." Early Muslims set before them one national ideal and proclaimed it in their prayers:

> *Our prayers and supplication, our life and death, are all for none but the Cherisher of the Worlds* (The Qur'án, 6:162).

The Muslims of the East and the West, the North and the South, all had one and the same ideal before them, and it was through this unity of ideal as a nation that they overcame the inherent prejudices of race, country and colour and made lightning progress in all walks of life, and established a universal brotherhood among themselves.

Prayer not only sets an ideal, but also takes it to the heart of every member of the nation, and thus secures for that ideal great moral and spiritual as well as material strength. When the whole nation backs an ideal it comes into practice more generally, and as strenuous efforts are made by each individual its realization becomes easier and more assured.

There is a saying: "If two hearts unite they can move a mountain." Young boys, little girls, grown-up men and women all take up an ideal set by prayer. That ideal is sure to be realized as a national ideal. But human ideal should be universal—common to all nations. World-fraternity and good should be the human ideal, and human prayers should help in achieving it.

It is a pity that humanity as a whole has not yet realized the value of prayers as a great asset to the progress of the world. Each nation, each people, seems to have monopolized that One Being who is the Creator, Evolver, Cherisher and Sustainer of all the nations of the world, of every age, country, race, colour and creed. We notice that His natural bounties are for all His creatures. The same elements, the same air, water, fire, etc., are for the use and benefit of all peoples. The starts, the sun, the moon, the sea, the land, the fruits, are at the disposal of all people. God is universal and impartial in all His bounties. If we all seek communion with Him; if we all have been created by Him; if we all try to do His will as represented by His work in Nature, why then do we not all, the whole humanity, Pray to Him and Him alone, and thus confirm the community of interest of the whole humanity?

PRAYERS AS A MEANS OF BRINGING THE WHOLE OF HUMANITY BEOFRE ONE CREATOR

Prayers can be constituted to be the means of bringing the whole of humanity before One Creator. The ideal of humanity can be made one. Then perhaps we shall have no more of such catastrophes as mankind passes through every now and then in blood and fire, a curse to civilization and culture, a disgrace to humanity itself.

If through prayers to a common Creator and Cherisher the idea is impressed on the minds of the people of all races and countries and creeds that the whole humanity is one brotherhood, that it has come from one and the same Source, that it goes back to the same, these ideas of the world-domination by one nation, this oppression of the weak by the stronger nations, these colour and racial prejudices, may cease to exist and these terrible wars might come to an end. God's earth is wide enough for all people. There is sustenance in it for all people. What is wanted is to engrave in human mind the idea of toleration and of goodwill. Prayers can do it.

If there is one God, then we should all pray to Him, and in Him we must all meet. What an amount of progress the world would see, what an amount of happiness would accrue to the whole world, if the whole of humanity would only realize its common brotherhood, and would call on one Cherisher and Creator in its prayers!

It is true that prayer has already played a part in the progress of the world. The nearer we come to our age, the more universal we find the character of the prayers. The horizon of human eye has extended. Tribal and racial deities are not invoked. The idea of universal brotherhood has gained ground. The Christian Lord's Prayer is universal. The *Fatihah of the Muslims is more wonderful. It runs thus*

> *"In the name of God, the compassionate, the Moralful*
> *"Praise be to God, Lord of the worlds!*
> *"King of the Day of Reckoning!*
> *"Thee only do we worship, and to Thee do we cry for help,*
> *"Guide us on the straight path,*
> *"The path of those to whom Thou has been gracious with whom Thou art not displeased, and who go not astray"* (The Qur'án, 1:1-7).

PRAYERS AS CONCEIVED BY ISLAM ARE A MEANS OF CREATING A WORLD BROTHERHOOD OF MAN

It is also true that because Muslims have stuck to their prayers in one language (Arabic) and to one Book (the Qur'án) all the Muslims of the world, whether they be in India or in China, or in America or in Australia, or anywhere else, understand each other in the Mosque, and thus territorial boundaries have been done away with. In every Mosque of the world the language spoken is the same. This has increased the feelings of fraternity in the Muslim nation spread all over the world. It must also be said to the credit of Islam, that it has tried to harmonize the people of the world with one another, and has thus contributed to the good and progress of the world. Prayers have played a prominent part in this world-harmonization.

Under the religious laws laid down by Islam, rich and poor Muslims of different races and colours meet together every Friday in Mosques and offer prayers without any distinction of place or position, under the leadership of any man elected by the assembly. Twice a year in a larger and more numerous congregation, all the Muslim residents of a town meet together to say their prayers and to embrace each other with fraternal affection. Every Muslim is enjoined to visit Mecca at least once in a lifetime, at a fixed time, in company with thousands of his brother Muslims, to offer his prayers. This great gathering, in which hundreds of thousands of true believers meet together from far and near at one central place, all wearing the same simple unsewn garment bare-headed, princes and peasants, from different countries and places, of various colours and races, standing shoulder to shoulder in their prayer, is an annual demonstration of Islamic Socialism, and sets a grand practical example of brotherhood and equality. In this gathering not the slightest difference can be noticed between a monarch and his subjects, a plebeian and a patrician. The idea bodly forces itself upon every mind that all human beings are one people, and that it is incumbent upon them to treat each other with perfect equality as members of the same brotherhood. This annual gathering demonstrates not only an outward and formal similarity and equality between man and man, but it also declares an identity of purpose and singleness of object on the part of all humanity. These myriads of men and women, old and young, come to that sea of sand bearing innumerable hardships, with only one purpose, one object, to pay homage to God, whom they can find everywhere, who is "Nearer to them than the vein of their neck", yet whom they love to proclaim at a common gathering as their common Deity—the one Cherisher of them all—the *Rabb alAlamín*. The idea in assembling this vast mass of humanity is to demonstrate at one and the same time common fraternity and spiritual affinity, the "Fatherhood" of God and brotherhood of man.

But this spirit requires still greater liberality and scope. The prayer to the "Lord of the worlds" should create a bound of fraternity with the people of the world of every creed who believe in Him.

"The Lord of the worlds" does not stand in need of human prayers. All His creation sings praises of Him and offers prayers to Him. Our prayers should do us good. They must help in the happiness and progress of the world.

Now that the world has realized that there is only *One* Being who deserves human worship and that over all creatures man is supreme; now that stone worship and star worship, and even man worship, are being abolished—even the Hindus proclaim that they are Monotheists; now that the world has been drawn closer together—distance is being shortened by every mode of conveyance: now that religious tolerance is also increasing among people of different places and creeds; it ought to be now not difficult to fix a place where representatives of all races and creeds could meet each other with fraternity, without the distinction of colour or nation, to offer their prayers to the One Cherisher and Lord of the whole universe for the Kingdom of Heaven on this earth—for peace and goodwill everywhere in the world. Political conferences for peace have failed. Wars, most deadly and inhuman wars, have raged in spite of the world peace conventions and conferences. It will be worth while to give prayer and faith a trial. The idea of common brotherhood of man can best be impressed by instituting common prayers to "the Lord of the whole universe." To send up prayers through Jesus Christ or Krishna is no good if prayers do not help us in becoming good and useful and progressive citizens of this world. Man wants salvation in this very world as well. Our prayers should mould our actions and make them of general beneficence and progress for our fellow-men.

The Purpose of Prayers

By our prayers we should be able to realize the needs of our fellow-beings. If we have something in our possession and the other person has not and needs it, we should be ready to give it to him. Do we not expect our God to give us what we do not posses and what He possesses? We must not forget:

> *Woe to those who pray,*
> *But in their prayers are careless*
> *Who make a show of devotion*
> *But refuse help to the needy* (The Qur'án, 107:4).

Nor this:

> *If thou bring thy gift to the altar and then rememberest that thy brother hath aught against thee, leave there thy gift before the altar, and go thy way; first be reconciled to thy brother, then come and offer thy gift.*

When we say our prayers we must not forget the real purport of those prayers. If we inspire ourselves with the same spirit in which we expect God to answer our prayers, if we also get determined to be beneficent as far as we can to others, what progress the world would make in every respect! Suppose some people labouring under bondage need education and suppose we can give that education, we should be willing to give it. Prayers ought to teach us to be selfless benefactors. If they are real, they must be beneficial not only to us but to the world at large. They must add to the progress and happiness of the world. Colour or social bars are fatal to the progress of the world. All humanity forms one nation.

When we pray we should be imbued with the spirit of the following immortal lines of a great American poet:

> "We owe allegiance to the State, but deeper, truer, more
> To the sympathies that God hath set within our spirit's core;
> Our country claims our fealty; we grant it so, but then,
> Before man made us citizens, great Nature made us men.
> He's true to God who's true to man: wherever wrong is done
> To the humblest and weakest 'neath the all-beholding sun,
> That wrong is also done to us; and they are slaves most base
> Whose love of right is for themselves and not for all their race.

God works for all, ye cannot have the hope of being free
With parallels of latitude, with mountain range and sea.
Put golden padlocks on Truth's lips, be callous as ye will,
From soul to soul o'er all the world, leaps one electric thrill."

The following is a soul-inspiring prayer, for every Muslim, from the Holy Qur'án, 2:206:

> *Our Lord! do not punish us if we forget or make a mistake. Our Lord! do not lay on us a burden as Thou didst lay on those before us. Our Lord! do not impose upon us that which we have not the strength to bear; and pardon us and grant us protection and have mercy on us. Thou art our Patron, so help us against the unbelieving people.*

Reference

1. Know Thyself.

[***By:*** *—Late Mushir Husayn Qidwa'i*
Source: *The Islamic Review & Arab Affairs, June 1970.*]

10

THE PROPHET MUHAMMAD'S MARRIAGES
(The Most Misunderstood Aspect of the Prophet's Life)

"O Prophet! say to your wives. If you desire this world's life and its ornature, then come, I will give you a provision and allow you to depart a goodly departure." (The Qur'án 33.28).

Khadíjah

The Prophet Muhammad's first marriage came about at the age of twenty-five with Khadíjah, who was then a widow of forty. Excepting his son Ibráhím, all the Prophet's children were born of Khadíjah. She passed away more than three years before the Hijrah (619 C.E). At the time of her death, the Prophet was fifty years old. Thus, the two lived together for not less than twenty-five years. Though it was a common practice in Arabia to have a number of wives, yet to the good old age of fifty, the Prophet had only Khadíjah as his wife.

'A'ishah

Khadíjah's loss weighed heavily upon the Prophet. Seeing this, one of his women Companions suggested that he should marry 'A'ishah, Abú Bakr's daughter, and then approached Abú Bakr on his behalf. The girl was one possessing exceptional qualities, and both Abú Bakr and the Prophet saw in her the great woman of the future, who was best suited to perform her duties of the wife of a teacher whose words and deeds had to be preserved for the guidance of mankind. But there were two difficulties in the way. The first was that 'A'ishah was already betrothed to Jubayr, and so Abú Bakr could not agree until the matter was settled with Jubayr. But Jubayr himself wanted now to get out of the engagement, as the gulf between Muslims and non-Muslims had by now widened to such a degree that the match was undesirable. The other difficulty was that 'A'ishah had not yet attained majority. This was solved by the postponement of the consummation of marriage till 'A'ishah reached the age of majority. And thus the marriage ceremony that was gone through amounted virtually to a betrothal. It was on the ninth of Shawwál in the tenth year of the Call (620 C.E).

'A'ishah's age

I may here take occasion to remove the popular misconception as to 'A'ishah's age. That she had not attained majority is clear enough, but that she was not so young as six years of age is also true. In the first place, it is clear that she had reached an age when betrothal could have taken place in the ordinary course, and must therefore, have been approaching the age of majority. Again, the Isábah, speaking of the Prophet's daughter Fátimah, says that she was about five years older than 'A'ishah. It is a well-established fact, that Fátimah was born when the Ka'bah was being rebuilt, i.e., five years before the Call (605 C.E.). 'A'ishah was therefore, born in the year of the Call or a little before it, and she could not have been less than ten years at the time of her marriage with the Prophet Muhammad in the tenth year of the Call (619 C.E.). This conclusion is borne out by the testimony of 'A'ishah herself, who is reported to have related that when the chapter of the Qur'án known as the "the Moon" (the 54th chapter) was revealed, she was a girl playing about and that she remembered certain verses then revealed. Now the fifty fourth chapter could not have been revealed later than the fifth year of the Call, and therefore, the report which states her to have been six years old in the tenth year of the Call when her marriage ceremony was gone through, cannot be correct, because this would show her to have been born about the time of the revelation of the 54th chapter. All these considerations show her to have been not less than ten years old at the time of her marriage. And as the period between her marriage and its consummation was not less than five years, because the consummation took place in the second year of the Flight, it follows that she could not have been less than fifteen at that time. The popular account that she was six years at marriage and nine years at the time of consummation is decidedly not correct, because it supposes the period between the marriage and its consummation to be only three years, and this is historically wrong.

Saudah

As stated above, 'A'ishah being very young at the time of her marriage, and the consummation having been postponed for some years, the Prophet married Saudah, a widow of advanced age, in the same year, i.e., the tenth year of the Call. She had emigrated along with her husband, to Abyssinia. On their return, her husband died on the way, leaving her in a terrible state of destitution. Small as the Muslim brotherhood then was, where could she look for a respectable shelter? So she offered her hand to the Prophet, who accepted it.

Hafsah, Zaynab, Umm Salamah

Hafsah, the daughter of 'Umar, was left a widow at the battle of Badr, her husband, Khunays, having been slain in action. 'Umar approached Abú Bakr and then 'Uthmán to take his daughter in marriage. This shows the dearth of marriageable men among the Muslims at the time. Both of them excused themselves, perhaps for the reason that Hafsah had a somewhat harsh temper. At last the Prophet took her in marriage in the year 3 A.H. (624 C.E.). The same year 'Abd Alláh Ibn Jahsh having fallen on the field of Uhud, his widow Zaynab was also taken in marriage by the Prophet. A year later, on the death of Abú Salamah, to his widow Umm Salamah was also extended the shelter of the Prophet's household.

Zaynab, Zayd's Divorced Wife

Zaynab was the daughter of the Prophet's aunt Umaimah, daughter of 'Abd al-Muttalib. The Prophet proposed to her brother that she should be given in marriage to Zayd, his own liberated slave. Both brother and sister were averse to this, for Zayd was only a freed man and as such could not, according to the pre-Islamic notions of respectability, enter into a matrimonial alliance with a woman of high birth such as Zaynab was. They desired the Prophet himself to marry her, but yielded under pressure from the Prophet who was anxious to abolish false distinctions of birth and class. The union, however, was not a happy one. Differences arose and relations were strained to breaking point. When all attempts at reconciliation had failed, there was only one alternative left—divorce. Thus, as a last resort they were separated. She was thereafter taken into marriage by the Prophet himself, that being the wish of Zaynab and her relations; and now that the marriage arranged by him had proved unsuccessful, he was morally bound to meet their desire. This marriage came about in the year 5 A.H. (626 C.E.).

Juwayriyyah

The same year, at the battle of Banú Mustaliq, a large number of prisoners, male as well as female, fell into the Muslim's hands. Among them was one Juwayiryyah, the daughter of an Arab chief, Hárith. Coming to the Prophet to ransom his daughter, he embraced Islam along with his two sons. Juwayriyyah's husband had already died. So Hárith consented to her marriage, the prisoners of Banú Mustaliq, about a hundred families, were all released by the Muslims. The tribe which was so honoured by the Prophet's relationship, they said, should not remain in captivity.

Umm Habibah

Among the emigrants to Abyssinia was also the daughter of Abú Sufyán, Umm Habíbah. Her husband, 'Ubayd Alláh, turned Christian there. On his death, while Umm Habíbah was yet in Abyssinia, the Prophet married her. She came to Medina in 7 A.H. (628 C.E.).

Safiyyah, Mary and Maymúnah

At the battle of Khaybar in 7 A.H. (628 C.E.), Safiyyah, the daughter of a Jewish chief, was one of the prisoners taken. Her husband had already fallen in action. The Jews had been a ceaseless source of trouble to the Muslims. The Prophet thought a matrimonial alliance with them might once and for all put a stop to their mischief. Thus Safiyyah joined the Prophet's wives. In this very year Mary, the Copt, who was sent as a present to the Prophet by Maqauqis, also joined the Prophet's household. She gave birth to a son, named Ibráhim. The same year another widow, Maymúnah, offered her hand to the Prophet, and it was accepted.

Polygamy is met with among the righteous

Why the Prophet contracted so many marriage relations is a question which disturbs many a mind. And there are men who do not hesitate to call him a profligate, simply because he resorted to polygamy. The man who brought about the most thorough transformation of a nation within twenty years; who, alone and unaided, swept away vice and immorality from a whole country, where the most strenuous efforts of powerful missionary nations had hopelessly failed; who by his personal example purified the lives of vast numbers of humanity—could such a man himself be in the grip of sin. An impure man could not consistently preach virtue; how could he take others by the hand and free them from bondage of sin, and inspire his very soldiers and generals with sentiments of virtue? Could a man who himself groped in the dark lead others to light? Whatever may be the views on polygamy of a world itself sunk deep in immoral practices, there is not the least doubt that plurality of wives is met with in the lives of many great religious personages, who by a consensus of opinion led lives of transcendent purity. Abraham, who is held in reverence by more than half the world up to this day, had more wives than one. Similar was the case with Jacob, Mose and David among the Israelites, and with some of the famous and revered sages of Hindús. The example of Jesus is quite out of question, as according to the Gospels he did not marry, and if his example were followed, the world would come to an end before long. Yet it is true that these great sages were not led away by sensual desires to a polygamous life. Purity in all respects was the outstanding characteristic of their lives, and his fact alone is sufficient to condemn the attempt to defame them on the basis of their resorting to polygamy. What was their object in doing so, it is difficult to say at the present day, as their histories are generally enveloped in darkness, but as the life of the Prophet Muhammad can be read in the full light of history, we will take his case in detail.

FOUR PERIODS OF THE PROPHET'S LIFE

The life of the Prophet may be divided into four periods so far as his domestic life is concerned. Up to twenty-five, he is a celibate life; from twenty-five to fifty-four years, he had in a married state with one wife; from fifty-four to sixty he contracted several marriages; and lastly from sixty till his death, he did not contract any new marriage.

First period

The most important period to determine whether the Prophet was a slave to his passions is the period of celibacy. If he had not been a complete master of his passions, he could not have led, up to the age of twenty-five, the exceptionally haste and pure life, which won him the title of Ullamin (the Trustworthy), in a hot country like Arabia, where development must necessarily take place early and passions are generally stronger. His worst enemies could not point to a single blot on his character when challenged later (The Qur'án 10:16). Even according to William Muir in his *'The Life of Mahomet'*, London 1876, all authorities agree "in ascribing to the youth of Mahomet a modesty of deportment and purity, and purity of manners rare among the people of Mecca". Now youth is the time when passions run riot, and the man who is able to control his passions in youth, and that in celibracy, can not possibly be conveived as falling a prey to lust in his old age. Thus the first period of his life, his celibracy up to twenty-five years of age, is conclusive proof that he could never fall a prey to his passions. It should be noted in this connection that in Arab society at the time there was no moral sanction against immoral life, so it cannot be said that he was kept back from an evil course by the moral force of society. Profligacy was the order of the day; and it was among people who prided on loose sexual relations that the Prophet Muhammad led a life of transcendent purity, and therefore, all the more credit is led to his purity of character.

Second period

Take now the next period, the period of a monogamous married life. When twenty-five years of age, he married a widow, Khadíjah, fifteen years his senior, and led a life of utmost devotion with her till she died, when he was fifty years of age. Now polygamy was the rule in Arabia at the time; and the wife had no cause of complaint, nor did she ever grumble, if the husband brought in a second or third wife. Marriage with Khadíjah had enriched him, though polygamy in Arabia was not limited to the rich; the poor as well resorted to it. The wife being a helpmate in the real sense of the word, because she helped the husband in earning his livelihood, as the woman generally does in the labouring classes, the poor had nothing to lose by resorting to polygamy. The Prophet belonged to the noblest family of the Quraysh, and if he had chosen to marry another wife it would have been quite easy for him. But he led a monogamous life of the utmost devotion to his wife during all this while. When Khadíjah died, he married a very elderly lady named Saudah, whose only recommendation for the honour was that she was the widow of a faithful companion of his, who had to flee to Abyssinia from the persecutions of the Quraysh. The main part of his life, from twenty-five to fifty, was thus an example for his followers that monogamy was the rule in married life.

Third period

Now comes the third period. In the second year of the Flight, began the series of battles with the Quraysh and the other Arab tribes, which appreciably reduced the number of males, the breadwinners of the family. These battles continued up to the eighth year of the Flight (627 C.E.), and it was during this time that the Prophet contracted all the marriages which appear objectionable to the modern mind, but which neither friend nor foe looked upon with disapprobation at the time. And how could they do so, for they saw them as acts of compassion and not as indulgence of the passions? Even a Christian writer, E. Bosworth Smith in his *Muhammad and Mohammedanism,* London 1873 C.E., admits this when he says: "It should be remembered, however, that most of Muhammad's marriages may be explained, at least, as much by his pity for the forlorn condition of the persons concerned, as by other motives. They were almost all of them widows who were not remarkable either for their beauty or their wealth, but quite the reverse." And what other motives could there be? Let us looked facts straight in the face. The Prophet had now a young and beautiful wife in 'A'ishah in his house. None of the other wives whom he married later compared with her either in youth or beauty. Surely then it was not attraction for beauty that led to these marriages. And we have already seen that from youth till old age the Prophet remained a complete master of his passions. The man who could live in celibacy up to twenty-five years, and still have the reputation of a spotless character, who up to the age of fifty-four lived with a single wife, and this notwithstanding the fact that polygamy was more the rule than the exception at the time, and that a polygamous connection was not in the least objectionable—such a man could not be said to have changed all of a sudden after fifty-five, when old age generally soothes the passions even of those who cannot control their passions in youth. No other motive than compassion for the ladies who were given this honour can be attached to these marriages. If there had been any less honourable motive, his choice would have fallen on others than widows, and under the Arab custom a man in his position could have had plenty of youthful virgins.

Circumstances in which the Prophet lived

I have said that a change for the worse could not come over a man who had led an undoubtedly spotless life until he reached fifty-five. If the beauty of woman could not excite his passions in youth and lead him away from the path of rectitude, how could it lead him away in old age? And what were the circumstances in which he lived at Medina during these years? It was not a life of ease and luxury that he was leading at the time: it was not a life of hardness, because it was at this very time that he had to carry on a struggle of life and death with the enemies of Islam. Huge armies came to crush him and the small band of Muslims at Medina. The whole of Arabia was aflame against him. He was not secure for minute. Battles had to be fought in quick succession. Expeditions had to be arranged and sent, "Prophet of God! we are tired of being in arms day and night," his Companions would say to him; and he had to console them by telling them that time would come when a traveller would be able to go from one end of the country to the other without having any arms. Jews and Christians were his enemies along with idolaters. His best friends were falling sometimes in battles and sometimes by treachery. Is it possible for a man to lead a life of ease and luxury under such circumstances? Even if a man had a mind to lead a life of self-indulgence, which the Prophet according to all available evidence had not, this was not the opportune time for it. Under such circumstances of warfare, with enemies within Medina and enemies all around it, with the number of the Muslims being insignificantly small in comparison with the enemy, with the news of assaults by overwhelming numbers on all sides, even a profligate's life would be changed, to say nothing of a man of admitted purity of character, which no temptation could shake, turning into a profligate.

How he passed his nights

If the Prophet's days during this period were passed so strenuously, how did he pass the nights? He had a number of lawful wives, but did he spend his nights in enjoyment with them? There is the clearest evidence on record in the Holy Qur'án (73:1-4, 20) as well as the Hadíth, that he passed half the night, and sometimes even more than that, in praying to God and in reciting the Holy Qur'án while standing in prayer. He would stand so long that his feet would become swollen. Could such a man be said to be taking wives for self-indulgence, when the minutest details of his life as available to us show conclusively that it was a strenuous life farthest away from indulgence of every kind?

Simplicity of his life

Let us now take another point. Was any change really witnessed in the later phase of the Prophet's life when he became the ruler of a state? Bosworth Smith writes: "In the shepherd of the desert, in the Syrian trader, in the solitary of Mount Hirá, in the reformer, in the minority of one, in the exile of Medina, in the acknowledged conqueror, in the equal of the Persian Chosroes and the Greek Heraclius, we can still trace a substantial unity. I doubt whether any other man, whose external conditions changed so much, ever himself changed less to meet them: the accidents are changed, the essence seems to me to be the same in all."

From the cradle to the grave, the Prophet passed through a diversity of circumstances—a diversity which can hardly be met with in the life of a single man. Orphanhood is the extreme of helplessness, while kingship is the height of power. From being an orphan he climbed to the summit of royal glory, but that did not create the slightest change in his way of living. He lived on exactly the same kind of humble food, wore the same simple dress, and in all particulars led the same life as he led in the state of orphanhood. It is hard to give up the kingly throne and lead the life of a hermit, but it is far harder that one should wield the royal scepter and at the same time lead a hermit's life, that one should possess power and wealth, yet spend it solely to promote the welfare of others, that one should ever have the most alluring attractions before one's eyes, yet should never for one moment be captivated by them. When the Prophet actually became the ruler of a state, the furniture of his house was composed of a matting of palm leaves for his bed and an earthen jug for water. Some nights he would go without food. For days no fire would be lit in his house to prepare food, the whole family living only on dates. There was no lack of means to live a life of ease and comfort. The public treasury was at his disposal. The well-to-do among his followers, who did not shrink from sacrificing their lives for his sake, would have been only too glad to provide him with every comfort of life, had he chosen to avail himself of them. But worldly things carried little weight in his estimation. No mundane craving could ever prevail over him, neither in times of indigence nor of plenty. Just as he spurned wealth, power and beauty, which the Quraysh offered him when he was yet in a state of utmost helplessness, so did he remain indifferent to them when god granted him all these things out of His grace.

Prophet's wives led a simple life

Not only did he himself live the simplest life of a labourer, but he did not even allow wealth to have any attraction for his wives. Shortly after their immigration into Medina, the condition of the Muslims had changed, and they carried on a prosperous trade. The later conquests went further to add to the comforts of life which they enjoyed. Quite a human desire crept into the hearts of the Prophet's wives that, like other Muslim families, they too should avail themselves of their share of comforts. Accordingly they approached the Prophet in a body to prevail upon him to allow them their legitimate share of worldly comforts. Thereupon came the Divine injunction:

> *"O Prophet! say to your wives, If you desire this world's life and its ornature, come, I will give you a provision and allow you to depart a goodly departing. And if you desire God and His*

Messenger and the latter abode, then surely God has prepared for the doers of good among you a might reward." (The Qur'án 33:28, 29).

Thus they were offered alternatives. They could either have worldly finery, or remain in the Prophet's household. Should they decide to have the former, they would have plenty of what they wanted, but would forthwith forfeit the honour of being the Prophet's wives. Can this be the reply of a sensual man? Such a man would have done everything to satisfy the shims of the objects of his affection. Nay, he would himself have desired that his wives should wear the most beautiful dress and live in comfort. No doubt the Prophet cherished great love and regard for his wives. "The best of you," he is reported to have said, "is the one who treats his wife best." This illustrates his attitude towards womanhood. He had immense regard for the rights of women and was the champion of their cause. But when his wives came to him with what was apparently quite a legitimate demand to have more of finery and ornaments, they were coldly told that if they would have these things, they were not fit to live in the Prophet's household. Does anyone who is a slave to his passions disregard the wishes of his wives in such a matter? This shows beyond the shadow of a doubt how free the Prophet's heart was of all base and sensual thoughts. He was prepared to divorce all his wives rather than yield to what he regarded as unworthy of his wives—an inclination towards worldly things. It shows conclusively that the object of his marriage was anything but self-indulgence.

Protection of women was the underlying idea

Let us consider once more the historical facts which led the Prophet to take a number of wives within the short space of five years, from the 3rd year of Hijrah to the 7th (624-7 C.E.), while before that he passed nearly thirty years of his life in a monogamous state. This period coincides exactly with the period during which incessant war was carried on between Muslims and non-Muslims. The circle of Muslim brotherhood was at the time very narrow. The perpetual state of war created disparity between the male and the female population of society. Husbands having fallen on the field of battle, their widows had to be provided for. But bread and butter is not the only provision needed in such cases, as is supposed by certain short-sighted statesmen. Sex inclination is implanted in human nature, and the statesman who neglects sex requirements leads society to moral corruption, ending ultimately in the ruin of the whole nation. A reformer with whom morals are all in all could not content himself with making provision merely for the eating and drinking of the widows. The Prophet was anxious for their chastity to a far greater extent than their physical needs. It became, therefore, necessary to allow polygamy. This is the reason that he himself took so many women to wife during the period when war was raging. Nearly all of his wives were widows. Where self-indulgence is the motive, the choice does not fall on widows. They must needs have virginity for its gratification. And there are no dearth of virgins. It would have been an enviable privilege for any Muslim to be father-in-law of the Prophet. But the object was a far nobler one—the protection of the widows of his friends. In polygamy alone lay the moral safety of the Muslim society as it then was.

Political reasons

Again, certain political reasons also led to some of the marriages. This was the case in the marriage with Juwayriyyah, a lady belonging to the Banú Mustaliq: and such was also the case in the marriage with Safiyyah, the widow of a Jewish certain. The Prophet wanted to conciliate both tribes, and that was the only motive in these marriages.

Other considerations

The case of the marriage with Zaynab may, however, be specially noted here as calumny has been at work in this case. Zaynab was the Prophet's first cousin, being the daughter of his aunt. When she reached the age of majority, she was offered in marriage to the Prophet by her brother. But the Prophet wedded her to Zayd, a slave who he himself had kind and who was deeply attached to him. The couple could not, however, pull on together, and after a time Zayd wanted to divorce her. The Prophet dissuaded him, as plainly stated in the Holy Qur'án (The Qur'án 33:36, 37). But ultimately a divorce was found necessary. The divorced woman is generally looked down upon in popular estimation, and this was a case in which a freed slave divorced a lady of high birth. By taking such a divorced woman as his wife the Prophet wanted to remove the false notion that divorce degraded woman. Thus by this act, which he was normally bound, because the lady has been at first offered in marriage to him, he elevated the whole class of divorced women who should otherwise suffer lifelong humiliation in society. If he had any desire of self-gratification, or if he had any passion for the lady, he would not have refuse her when she was offered to him as a virgin. Refusal of her hand in the first instance, and taking her in marriage when, being divorced, she was lowered in general estimation, shows conclusively that his motive in this marriage was anything but self-gratification.

Fourth period

We now come to the fourth period. With the conquest of Mecca in the year 8 A.H. (629 C.E.), internal warfare came practically to an end. Disturbances there were, but on the whole peace had been established in the country and normal conditions were restored. And it is from the 8th year of the Flight to the end of his life, that we find that the Prophet did not contract any new marriage. What is the evidence of facts then? It is clearly this, that the Prophet added to the number of his wives only during the time that he had to live in a state of warfare when the number of males was reduced, so that many women would have been left without protection and without a home, if the difficulty had not been solved by permitting a limited polygamy. Before the Prophet had to enter on a defensive warfare, he lived in the company of a single wife, and after war was ended, he contracted no new marriage, and this sets all doubts at rest as to the motives of the Prophet. In all the marriages which he contracted during the war, there was some hidden moral end in view. Then arose situation in his life under which he could not, consistently with the moral and religious mission of his life, help taking more wives than one. In that, he only showed compassion to the weaker sex.

Prophet's natural liking was not for polygamy or war

Although living in a country in which polygamy was the rule, the Prophet had no liking for polygamy. He passed the prime of his life, up to 53 years of age, as the husband of a single wife, thus showing that the union of one man and one woman was the rule under normal conditions. But when conditions arose, he did not, like a sentimentalist, shirk his duty for the sake of an idea. He saw that the chastity of woman was at stake if polygamy was not allowed, and for the sake of a higher interest, he permitted polygamy as an exception to meet exceptional circumstances. Exactly thus, he had to resort to war, thought by disposition he was averse to it. Full forty years before the Call (610 C.E.), he had been living in a land where the sword was wielded as freely as a stick elsewhere, where fighting and feuds were the order of the day, where men would fly at each other's throats like wild animals, where there was no chance of survival for one who could not use the sword; yet not once during these forty years did he deal a blow at an enemy. The same was the case with him for fourteen years after the Call. That he was peace-loving by nature is shown by the clear injunctions relating to peace in the Holy Qur'án:

> *"And if they incline to peace, do thou also incline to it and trust in God.... And if they intend to deceive thee, then surely God is sufficient for thee."* (8:61, 62).

His acceptance of the truce of Hudaybiyah though its conditions were humiliating to Muslims, who were ready to lay down their lives one and all rather than accept those terms, is also a clear proof of his peace-loving nature. But when duty called him to take the field to save his community, he did not hesitate to take up the sword against an overwhelming majority. He acted as a sagacious general in all fields of battle, and behaved like a brave soldier when opportunity demanded. He knew how to disperse an enemy in time before it had gained sufficient strength to deal a severe blow at the Muslims. And once, in the battle of Hunayn, when his army was in flight owing to the severe onslaught of the enemy's archers, he alone was advancing towards the enemy, till his soldiers rallied round him. By disposition he had no inclination for war, yet circumstances arose which dragged him into the field of battle, and he then displayed the wisdom of a general and the bravery of a soldier. So by disposition he was not inclined to polygamy, living a celibate life of unexampled purity up to twenty-five years and a married life of a monogamous husband up to fifty-four, but when duty called him to take more women under his shelter, he answered the call of duty. It may be added in conclusion that the verse limiting the number of wives to four when a necessity for polygamy arose, was in all probability revealed after the Prophet had contracted those marriages, but he was expressly permitted to retain under his shelter all the woman whom he had married (The Qur'án 33:50), and he did not contract any marriages after the revelation of that verse (The Qur'án 33:52).

Reference

1. *Op. cit.*

[***By:*** *—Late Muhammad 'Ali*
Source: *The Islamic Review & Arab Affairs, February 1970.*]

11

THE BELIEF OF MUHAMMAD
(A STRUCTURAL ANALYSIS OF THE PROPHETHOOD)

The British Philosopher David Hume on the Meaning of the word Belief

The really powerful factor of Muhammad's mission from the beginning to the end, was his unshakable belief that he had been called by God. It was this conviction which exercises an incredible influence on others; and it is the certainty with which he came forward as the executor of God's will, which gave his words and ordinances an authority, which in the end proved compelling.

Certain Orientalists (like the Italian Prince Leone Caetani (d. 1926 C.E.)) wish to see this belief as the result of a long development and continued reflection. This is certainly not correct. We would much rather trust the Tradition, which tells of a sudden outburst of conviction that he was called to proclaim the word of God, and also the fact that he unselfishly endured years of hostility and humiliation in Mecca, which proves his unshakable conviction in his lofty task.

Belief is a term whose meaning is sufficiently understood by those who use it. In philosophy we can go farther and assert that it is something. The British philosopher David Hume [1] says that through belief we can distinguish the ideas of the judgment from the figments of the imagination. Belief is an act, or attitude of the mind, or as Hume sometimes describes it, it is a feeling or sentiment, through which the mind is carried in opinion though not in knowledge, to a causally active, preveniently existing, world of things and selves. It is by virtue of its capacity of so doing that it can similarly, in causal inferences, enable the mind not merely to expect or anticipate, but to believe in the existence of the inferred effect or cause. Causal inference, if it is to lead to real existence, must start from real existence (it is likewise so in the case of memory) and this is possible only if belief enters in this radical form into the experiences from which the inferences start. If any and every impression has an infective power, as Hume declares, it is not surprising that belief should know no proper bounds, and favoured as it is by man's essentially social make-up, should so spread in epidemic forms.

The profound effect of Muhammad's belief on others

Indeed Muhammad's belief spread epidemically over his family, neighbours, local citizens, all nations, and a great part of mankind, not only in his lifetime, but through centuries, and through continents, very often in unpredictable dimensions. This unpredictability was mentioned in the Holy Qur'án 10:100:

> *...Nobody can believe except by God's permission And He casts mental confusion on those who will not reason.*

In another verse it is stated (6:39):

> *Those who reject Our messages are deaf and dumb, in darkness. God leaves in error, whomsoever He pleases. And whom He pleases He guides him on the right path.*

More explicit is the verse (81:27-29):

> *It is a Reminder (the Qur'án) for the nations.—For such people who like to be righteous.—And you cannot be righteous (except) if God, the Lord of the worlds like it.*

What is the "Faith of Abraham," a phrase used in the Qur'án

Metaphysical determinism, defined in Islam as God's will, decided who will believe in the revelation and who will not. And this determinism has decided the belief of Muhammad as is expressed in the following verse (6:162):

> *Say! As for me my Lord has guided me to the right path—a right faith, the faith of Abraham, who was not a polytheist* (but an upright man).

From this verse we can presume that Muhammad believed in a faith, which was called the "Faith of Abraham", even before he got his own mission. The religion of Abraham called the *Hanifyyah* or *Hanafiyyah* is a religious movement, the historical development of which is wrapped in obscurity, which cannot be cleared up with the material at present available (a field for Muslim's research workers!).

The Holy Qur'án in its use of this word was simply following a recognized term, and it may be suggested a highly probable that the *Hanifiyyah*, even before Muhammad he, denoted the people, who, although influenced by Christianity, had rejected both Christianity and Judaism in favour of a simpler and uncomplicated faith, as is evident from the verse (3:66):

> *Abraham was not a Jew nor a Christian, but he was (an) upright (man), Muslim, and he was not a polytheist.*

It is clear here that the word hanif means an original, intuitive, simple faith in contrast to polytheism on the one hand and the, in part, corrupt religion of the possessors of the Old Scriptures. Some orientalists, like the German Wellhausen, achieve that the word hanif originally meant a Christian abectic (*al-'a'bid al-mutahannif*) who observes prayers. In Aramaic (Syriac) "hanifu" or "hanfe" is a description for Sabians.[2]

In West Aramaic (Canaanite) "hanef" means: hypocrite, godless, heathen, heretic. For this reason one German orientalist, Schulthesis, has pointed out that the Aramaic "hanef" or "hanfa" cannot be the Arabic *hanif.* If we remember that the Canaanites were polytheists, and that for them a man who is not a polytheist is a "godless fellow", we assume that the word "hanef" was for them a designation of those people who did not follow their religion.

Muhammad's belief before the Revolution came to him

Muhammad, before the Revelation came to him, believed in a simple monotheistic religion. He was evidently practising the precepts of this faith, which can be deduced from the fact that he was leading an anchroetic life in certain seasons of years, when he used to go into retreat in the wilderness for meditation. There is no historical evidence of the time when Muhammad adhered to this religion, but from the following verses we can deduce that after perplexity and erring, Muhammad was enlightened to the right belief (The Qur'án 93:6-8):

> *Did He not find you an orphan and give (you) protection? And He found you erring so He guided (you) on the right path? And He found you in need, so He enriched you!*

These three phases in the life of Muhammad are well known. Early in his life he became an orphan, but his uncle gave him shelter and protection. He was very poor before he married Khadíjah, and after this marriage he became a merchant. His acceptance of the Faith of Abraham must, according to the Qur'án, be in chronological order, between those two events: when he became an orphan and before his 25th birthday when he married. It can be probable that he had already embraced this Faith when he with his uncle was travelling for the first time to Syria, where on the way he encountered a Christian monk who recognized in him signs of exceptional wisdom. The myth about corporeal stigmata suggesting his future vocation are certainly aprocryphal, because all known texts from the Old and New Testament do not contain such references, and the Qur'án never recognized any Gnostic Scriptures as authentic and valid. Anyhow, this journey was at the time when he was 9-12 years old, and that signifies that he had become a monotheist even before his puberty. His belief in the one Creator and Divine Presence, must have already been established at that time, but we can realize how difficult it was for him to accept his own mission when his vocation came. The Holy Qur'án insists that not only Muhammad, but no other mortal has ever had a direct confrontation with Almighty God (The Qur'án 43:51):

> *It is not granted to a mortal that God should* (directly) *speak to him, except by intuition or (the like) from behind a veil, or by sending a messenger* (who) *reveals after His permission* (what) *pleases Him. Surely He is High and Wise.*

How the Revelation came to the Prophet Muhammad

The Revelation to Muhammad came by this last way (The Qur'án 43:52):

> *Also We (give) you revelation (by intermediary of) a spirit acting (according) to our orders. You ignored (at that time) Old Scriptures as well as (any common) Faith. But We made (Our revelation as a) light, (by which) We guide whom We please of Our servants. And you surely He guides to the right path.*

The spirit, which brought the Message to Muhammad, was the Angel Gabriel, as is evident from the following verse (2:97):

> *Say: (Who can be) an enemy to Gabriel?—(and it is) he (who) revealed it (The Qur'án) to your (subliminal) mind by God's permission, verifying that which (was revealed) before it and (as a) guidance and good news for the believers.*

The Holy Qur'án describes angels with the word Malá'ikah, which is the Arabic broken plural of an early Semitic (Canaanite) word *malak* meaning "messenger". Indeed the Holy Qur'án uses the word "messenger" as an alternative name for angel. It was one of these spirit-messengers with a personal name Gabriel, who appeared to Muhammad during his retreat and meditation in a cave on Mount Hirá, and showed him a piece of cloth on which certain verses were written, saying:

> *Read!*

When Muhammad protested that he could not read, the spirit-messenger pressed him so strongly that he was nearly suffocated. At the third repetition, the spirit-messenger pronounced the five first verses of the Quran (96:1-5):

> *Read in the name of your Lord, Who creates (everything); (He) creates (also) man from worm. Read (because) your Lord is most Generous. (It is He) Who taught (man writing) by the pen. (He) taught man what he knew not!*

And these verses Muhammad retained fast in his memory.

The period of fatrah or intermission in the Revelation

During the following six months there was a total absence of any communication, a period called in Muslim history "intermission" (in Arabic, *fatrah*), an interval which was much more painful to Muhammad than any other event in his life. He was searching meanwhile for an explanation of his first psychic experience: the apparition of this unusual spirit-messenger, his strange voice and the wonderful message he was bringing forth. He was anxious and wanted to know what significance all this had, if any. His belief in the one of God instinctively was firm, and the spirit-messenger had spoken in the name of that God, but was it a reality or an illusion? His wife consulted one of her relatives named Waraqah Ibn Nawfal, a Christian whose adherence to a particular church is not yet established.

Nawfal said that this spirit-messenger could be the "greatest Námús",[3] who used to come to Moses, and in that case, he added, Muhammad was the prophet of that era. In that epoch psychic experiences were familiar in Arabia. Many people who were witnessing apparitions or hearing voices, or producing the phenomena of direct voices, were supposed to be possessed by the so-called "djinns", which are in our modern terminology earth-bound spirits with a low average intelligence, and endowed with passions and drives. These possessed people in Arabia were despised as abnormals and psychopaths. This was exactly the label that many of his enemies applied to Muhammad later! After his first psychic experience, Muhammad did probably himself imagine that he was possessed. He gradually assumed confidence and had a full moral recovery after the second revelation (The Qur'án 74:1-2) which opens with:

> *O wrapped one! Arise and warn!*

During his Mission, the revelation came to Muhammad in the form of clairaudience (the voices ringing as a bell), or in the form of clairvoyance, in which he observed a messenger looking like a young man who spoke to him. Very rarely a full materialization of a young man occurred who was visible to others and whispered to him in the ear, or spoke loudly with him in front of other people (*vide* Bhukhárí, The *Sahíh*, Fadá'il al-Qur'án, Chapter 1; Ibn Hishám, *Sírah Rasúl Alláh*). I repeat again that there was never a direct confrontation with Almighty God either by hearing or visualization mentioned.

According to a Tradition (*Mukhtasar al-' Ajá'íb* (Abrégé des Merveilles)) translated by the French Orientalist Carré de Vaux, p. 9, the Prophet Muhammad asked the spirit-messenger Gabriel, "Have you ever seen your Lord?" Gabriel was troubled and replied, "O Muhammad! Between Him and Me there are seventy thousand veils of light; if I approached a single one of these veils. I should be consumed!" If this Tradition is authentic, there is also not a direct confrontation between Gabriel and Almighty God, but he (Gabriel) too got his knowledge by intuition. Looking on the whole situation from this perspective, Muhammad had to believe in an apparition coming to him at predictable intervals, and speaking to him as a messenger of God, and therefore, Muhammad is (indirectly) God's messenger to mankind.

To believe this complex chain of events is far beyond the normal human capacity. If we assume that belief is an act of mind, being a distinctive, though not separable type of feeling or sentiment, we can say that it must be innate and not acquired by conditioning. The Holy Qur'án 10:100 says exactly the same thing:

> *And nobody can believe, except by God's permission. And He casts mental confusion on those who will not reason.*

The purpose of belief in moral judgment, as stated in Qur'ánic verses, is to alter or confirm and generally to control, the behaviour of people. This is achieved by building up attitudes in man, by forming his "character", and thus determining his choice. But since it is the believer's actions that we are interested in, there is no point in determining an attitude or choice, if this does not in turn determine an action. And only because of the harmony between an intuitive belief—metaphysically determined—and the revealed message (The Qur'án 30:30) says:

> *So follow only an upright religion, the natural one, made by God, in which He has created men. There is no altering (in) God's creation—that is the right religion but most people ignore it.*

The effect of the Prophet Muhammad's message in the world

Muhammad and the people who believed in his message became a community, a nation, and a force which changed the history of mankind. The belief is beyond intellect, it is a kind of emotion, and emotion always needs to be stabilized. One stabilizing factor is opposition, the second is the reasonable verification of the alleged facts, and the third is the realization of predicted events. All these three factors can be found in Muhammad's life. He was confronted to the utmost mostly with unjust claims, and under false pretensions, and very often completely senseless. All his conviction that he was on the right path. Muhammad was very well aware of the limitations of his personal education and knowledge. Being a genuine believer in God, he was sceptic in accepting or studying any other religion, be it traditional, polytheistic, Christian Jewish. If he had any notion concerning those religions, especially their history and controversies, it must have been very rudimentary. The Revelation on the contrary was rich in details concerning the Old Scriptures, and was decisive in several controversial points, giving sometimes absolutely original explanations for the very complicated problems.

After a verification of the different themes from the Revelation with the people who are devoted to the study of the Old Scriptures, Muhammad's belief as well as the belief his followers was certainly reinforced. Just to mention one verses of the Qur'án 10:94, concerned with this matter:

> *But if you are in doubt as to that which We have revealed to you, ask those who know the previous Scriptures. Certainly the Truth has come unto you from your Lord, so be not a sceptic.*

The third and most important reinforcing factor is the realization of the predicted events. To understand pre-cognition is not possible without acceptance of the doctrine of metaphysical determinism. Moreover, pre-cognition cannot be apprehended without contact with the source of creation's planning. Therefore, pre-cognition is the basis of prophecy, and prophethood or the fundamental conception of Islam as the Faith. Several prophecies, many of which we ignore today, were realized during the lifetime of Muhammad. All those realizations did increase the belief of Muhammad in his spirit-control Gabriel, and the trust in the message Gabriel was bringing to him, and through him to humanity. The evolution of Muhammad's belief has two phases: first, his early youth, when he intuitively abhorred the existent establishment of polytheism, and the distorted revealed religions of Judaism and Christianity, while at the same time he believed in one God, the Almighty, and present everywhere, and tried to know Him better through meditation and ascetism. This phase certainly prepared the coming of the next phase, which followed after the apparition of the spirit-messenger Gabriel—that he was a messenger of God whom Muhammad had already conceptualized—and that that message he (Muhammad) was to give to mankind.

In spite of the fact that belief is a function of mind, this experience is rather mystical than rational, even if we find both of them (mystical and rational) sometimes intermingled. Therefore, belief is a subject of unconsciousness the same as intuition, and only by an unknown mechanism of conversion would be translated into consciousness. We are aware of it, but how it comes to us we do not know. When we reason why all this is so, realist is often eager to argue that everything happens because of a "real" necessity or connection between the events, which serves to make all actual sequences intelligible. In this sense we can understand this Tradition: "If your existence (O Muhammad!) was not pre-planned, I (God) will never have created the Cosmos."

References

1. David Hume (1711-1776 C.E.)—British philosopher, historian economist and essayist, who conceived of philosophy as the inductive science of human nature. In his published works: (1) Treatise of Human Nature; (2) Essays, Moral and Political; (3) Three Essays, Moral and Political; (4) Philosophical Essays Concerning Human Understanding; (5) Dialogues Concerning Natural Religion, he treats the problem of belief, intuition and natural (instinctive) religion.
2. Sabians—This name has been given to two quite distinct sects. (a) Mandeans or Subbas, followers of Eastern Gnostic religions. They consider the Biblical saints as false prophets including Abraham, Moses and Solomon. According to them a true prophet was Yahyá, son of Zacharia. He used baptism (to plunge, or to immerse) which in Hebrew has "S—b' " for its root, and from this root the name Subba is derived. According to their holy book Ginzah (Treasury), Yahyá baptized by mistake a false prophet. Yishu Meshiha (Jesus?), son of the devil (Ruha Kadishta). The false Messiah was crucified and his city—Jerusalem—was destroyed.

   (b) The Sabaeans of Harran, a pagan sect worshipping stars, which survived a considerable period under Muslim rule.
3. Námús—In Greek and Arabic means: "the trusted one, confider of a secret". Tabari says that the "greatest námús" is a gloss for Gabriel. According to the lkhwán al-Safá (the Brethren of Purity it appeared to Adam, and lastly, to Moses and to Jesus. We are told in the Holy Qur'án 79:2, that Jesus predicted the advent of a Prophet whose name was Ahmad. In the Gospel of John 14:16, 16:7, and 16:12-14, we have mention of the "Spirit of Truth", or Paraclete, which is the Greek word for the Comforter. In the original language of the Gospels, Aramaic, it is designated as al-manahmana. It is true we cannot know what was the original

word, because the Gospel of St. John was originally written in Greek, and not like that of St. Mathew in Aramaic. Three Synoptical Gospels do not mention the advent of the Paraclete. The other designation of Gabriel, or his Message in the Holy Qur'án is Sakinah, which is a corruption of the Hebrew word Shekinah 9:26, 40. 48:4. 18, 26. In the Old Testament Ruah Hakkodesh (the Holy Spirit), which rests of the prophets, gradually develops of the Shekinah. So we find that Muslim writers also use Sakinah occasionally for the "Holy Ghost".

The word Shekinah in Hebrew means "Dwelling". Rabbinic teaching explains it as the majestic presence or manifestation of God, which has descended to "dwell" among men. To avoid the anthropomorphic expressions in the continuously changing Bible new Aramaic expressions were introduced instead of Shekinah Menora (logos) or Yekara-Kalod (glory), which means presence glory or holiness. In all these statements the Shekinah identical with the Holy Spirit. The *Shekinah* tinkled like a bell (Sotah 96), while the Holy Spirit also manifested itself to human senses in light and sound. In a Prophetic Tradition (vide Bhukhari, the Sahih, Ba'd al-Wahy, Chapter 2) we are told: "Sometimes it comes as the ringing of a bell; this kind is the most painful. When it ceases, I retain what was said. Sometimes it is an angel who speaks to me as a man, and I retain what he says."

Two arks came out of Egypt with Israel—one containing the Shekinah (here the meaning is the Scrolls with the Message of the Holy Spirit), and the other the mummy of Joseph. In the Holy Qur'án 2:248, it is said:

And their prophet (Samuel) *said to them: The sign of* (Saul) *kingdom is that* (he will) *bring to you ark with the Sekina* (Scrolls of God's Message) *from your Lord and to the rest of things what remained from Moses and Aaron's followers, the angels bearing it. There is* (also) *a sign if you are believers.*

The ark mentioned in I Samuel 4:4 was drawn by bullocks. But due to the proverbial distortions of the Bible the real wording is lost. Here apparently a psychic phenomenon of apport is mentioned, of the lost ark with the relics of the Exodus, which are "apported" by spirit-messengers.

[***By:*** *—Dr. Mahmud Muftie*

Source: *The Islamic Review & Arab Affairs, February 1970.*]

12

The Battlefields of the Prophet Muhammad

Uhud

I

The Quraish of Mecca make preparations for attack on Medina after their defeat at Badr

The importance of the overland route to Syria and Egypt was too great for the Quraish of Mecca to abandon it at their first reverse at Badr. They did not find it an extravagance to collect contributions of a quarter of a million *Dirhams* towards preparation for a retaliatory expedition (*Sirah* of al-Sha'miy, ch.Uhud). They further spent practically as much in ransoming their seventy comrades taken prisoner by the Muslims at Badr. Each prisoner had to pay at an average 4,000 Dirhams as ransom money. Ibn Hisham (p. 555 ff.), *al-Sha'miy* (ch. Uhud), and others have recorded that the Quaraishites did not content themselves with their local voluntary militia, or even with the contingent of their perpetual, though mercenary, allies of the tribe of Ahabish. They sent important personalities, such as 'Amr Ibn al-'As, 'Abdallah Ibn al-Ziba'ra, Hubairah Ibn Wahb, Musafi 'Ibn 'Abd Manaf, Abu 'Azzah 'Amr Ibn 'Abdallah al-Jumahiy, to tour through all the tribes of Arabia and explain to them the new peril that was arising with Islam, and ask them to join forces in a "police action" against Medina. The mission was successful to a degree that "throngs of Bedouins assembled" for the task.

The secret agent of the Prophet at Mecca, his uncle 'Abbas, in spite of his being charged with ransom money when he was taken prisoner at Badr along with other Meccans, did not fail to inform the Prophet of the developments in time, by the agency of a Bedouin of the Ghifar tribe (*Ibn Sa'd*, II/ i p. 25; *al-Sha'miy, in loco*). Medina was thus prepared when the enemy advanced in the month of Shawwal of the year 3 A.H. (615 C.E.). The Quraish and their allies camped near Mount Uhud, north of the city of Medina.

Mount Uhud

Uhud is a mountain due north of Medina, about three miles from the centre of the city. The Quraishites came from Mecca, which, as everybody can see, lies far in the south of Medina. I was for long intrigued why the Meccan invaders, coming from the south, did not halt to the south of Medina in order to launch the attack on the city of the Prophet Muhammad, but marched on still further, by-passed Medina and camped to the north of the city, thus cutting their own way of retreat and reinforcement. I asked many a savant, local as well as foreign, and when nobody could satisfy me, I reluctantly concluded that the present Uhud must not have been the original Uhud where the famous battle was fought: the genuine Uhud must lie somewhere in the neighbourhood of Quba, now forgotten. The unanimous assurance of classical as well as modern historians and geographers even the tomb of Hamzah, the martyr par excellence of Uhud reputation, could not move me to conclude otherwise.

Yet, when I got the opportunity of visiting the site and studying the terrain, I understood what the turning of pages of scores of books for years past and talking to or corresponding with savants of unrivalled erudition could not explain to me.

The location of Medina and what it looked like during the days of the Prophet Muhammad

The fact is, Medina is situated in a lava plain, about ten miles long and as wide. This was originally called the plain (Jawf) of Medina, and later renamed "Haram" by the Prophet.

This plain is surrounded on all sides by chains of high mountains, and communications are maintained through narrow valleys. This plain, "between 'Air and Thawr" of the classical writers, is also not an even one: in between lie the majestic Mount Sal' and several other smaller hills of considerable strategic value.

In the time of the Prophet, Medina was not a city as its layout makes it today. It had not the congested streets and localities of modern towns. On the other hand, there lived in Medina in those days several Arab and Jewish tribes, and the locality or village of each tribe was separated from others, and lay at a distance of one, two or more furlongs from each other. A chain of such villages was to be seen from Mount 'Air right up to Mount Thawr.

These tribal villages each possessed one or more water wells, and the dwelling houses were constructed of stone and were generally double storeyed. Every village possessed several strong towers, called indifferently *Utm* or *Ajamah*. In time of war, women, children, cattle and other movable goods were removed to them for safety. At one time there were more than one hundred such towers in the city, and the Banu Zaid alone possessed fourteen of them (*Diwan* of Qais Ibn al-Khatim, ed. Rowalski, p. 18). Some of them were very big. So the Utm al-Dihyan, belonging to Uhaihah Ibn al-Julah, was, according to *Kitab al-Aghani* (XIII, 124) a three-storied building; its ground floor was constructed of the black lava stone, and the two upper storeys (*nabarah*) were of stones "white as silver"; and the tower was so high that one could see it from a distance of a day's journey on camel. In the vicinity of Quba, the ruins of this tower were still to be seen in 1947. Its ground floor is preserved, and even in its ruined form gives us an opportunity of seeing a monument of military architecture of pre-Islamic days in Medina. Inside these towers there were often wells, so that in case of prolonged siege, drinking water should not be lacking to the inmates.

Apart from these dispersed and widely-separated villages, there were in Medina gardens and farms belonging to individuals in each tribe. Their compound walls were generally built of stones. Such gardens were spread in all directions, in and around Medina.

Among these tribal habitations, one was called Yathrib. The hamlet is still remembered, and is shown to have existed south-west of Mount Uhud, where water abounds. May be this was most prosperous, or in some other way most important or even the earliest conglomeration there in pre-Islamic times. Anyhow, it gave its name to the whole town, an appellation of the whole by the name of its part, a phenomenon not seldom come across in other countries. The township of Madinah al-Nabiy, later simply Madinah (Medina), lies in the centre of the municipal area.

The Meccan Quraishites had no particular grudge against the general population of Medina; they were angry against only one person, their co-citizen, the Prophet Muhammad, who had taken refuge there. To reach the "Madinah of the Prophet", it was necessary to cross thick clusters of trees of numerous gardens, and there was no open space to serve as a battlefield for an army of several thousand on either side. In his *Wafa al-Wafa* (s.v. Khandaq), al-Samhudiy quotes from the second century author, Ibn Ishaq, that "one side of Medina was exposed and the rest of the sides were strongly protected by buildings and date-palm groves through which an enemy could not get access".

The terrain around Medina

Judging from present-day topography of the region of Medina, in the south-east, Quba and 'Awali' were thickly populated. In the south-west and south, the lava and extremely uneven hilly terrain was absolutely useless as a fighting ground both for infantry and cavalry. In east the Jewish villages succeeded one another from Quba to Uhud. In the west also there are plantations and gardens, though not so thickly clustered. The ground is less fertile and the condition could not have been better in those days. The assembly hall of the tribe of the Banu Sa'idah is shown on the northern wall of the modern town, just to the east of the Sha'miy Gate. This tribe must have lived there. Beyond the north-eastern Majidi Gate, there are other very old gardens, with reminiscences of the time of the Prophet Muhammad. Mid-north, dozens of old wells were recently discovered when ground was being cleared for the construction of the general hospital. A bit farther to the west, on the very Mount Sal' the Banu Haram have left their tribal graveyard, and apparently they lived then in that direction. All along the west, along the river bed of Wadi al-'Aqiq especially in the north-west, down to the historic well of Bi'r Ru'mah and even further south to the mosque of two Qiblahs (*Qiblatain*) there are numerous gardens. The Bi'r Ru'mah and the land watered thereby originally belonged to a Jew, and 'Uthman (later the third Caliph) purchased it at the instance of the Prophet and made of it a public bequest, as is well known.

Thus only the far north offers an open space. The white saline earth is unfit for cultivation of any kind, even today. The cultivation of any kind, even today. The locality where the Prophet Muhammad lived was more vulnerable from this side than from any other.

As mentioned above, south of Medina is hilly and full of lava blocks, and communications are maintained there through deep valleys and gorges. The route leading to the city from this direction and passing by Quba is rather difficult, and is reported never to have been used by big caravans. Single individuals scale it rarely, in an emergency only. Apparently the Prophet Muhammad himself had come that way, are the time of migration, for reasons of security; for he came first to Quba, and later moved to the middle town. But the horses and animals of transport of a large army would not use it. Moreover, it was the hot season at the time of the battle of Uhud, and the sun rendered the lava too hot even for camels.

Camels never like stony ground. Lava plains surround Medina from the south, from the east and the west; only the north is immune from it. Houses were certainly built in the lava plain, apparently as a security measure, yet no plantations are possible there. An army camp required grazing lands, which are not found there. Any army may cross somehow the lava plain yet would not select it for a battleground. It is to be remembered that the 'Anbariyal paratively recent construction, about three hundred years. Otherwise, in ancient times, the caravans from the south halted we are assured, at Dhu 'l-Hulaifah, and then entered the bed of Wadi al -'Aqiq, and, leaving Medina to their right, traversed northwards as far as the confluence of the Zaghabah, and then alone turned back to Medina. The soft sand of the river bed was liked by the camels.

Such were the physical impediments of the terrain, which forced the Meccan army, tired and almost dead after the arduous march of twelve continuous days, to get away from Medina and camp at a safe distance from the enemy and take the much needed rest for men and for animals. In the locality of Zaghbah there is water and grass. The Meccans were sure of their victory, and so they did not worry about the route of their return.

A description of the terrain of Mount Uhud

As mentioned previously, Mount Uhud lies to the north of Medina, and stretches in a straight line in an east-westerly direction. It is four to five kilometres in length. Just in the middle portion, facing the town, there is a natural curve, semi-circular or horse-shoe in shape, spacious enough to hold several thousand people. There is another open space further inside, and both of these are connected by a narrow passage. To the south of Uhud flows the Wadi Qanat, to the south of which stands the 'Ainain Hill, also called the "Hill of the Archers" (*Jabal al-Rumat*) on account of the archers posted on it by the Prophet on the day of the battle of Uhud. In the spacious open ground, north of Wadi Qanat, there are two springs. May be the name of Hill 'Ainain (lit., *two springs*) is due to this fact.

Preparation of the Muslims, who were only 700 strong, to meet the enemy, 3,000 strong

When the Quraishite army arrived in Dhu 'l-Hulaifah, Muslim spies mingled with the marching hordes, and returned to report to the Prophet Muhammad only when the enemy stopped and encamped at the Zoghabah, west of Uhud (*Isti'ah*, § Anas Ibn Fudalah; the *Maghazi* of Waqidiy, fol. 49b). The Prophet Muhammad was personally disposed to defend the city from inside "and fight it out in the streets", courting a siege, yet the clamour of the younger officers at last decided him to go out of the city and join battle in the open (*Ibn Hisham*, p. 558). He asked the volunteers to assemble in front of the Twin Towers of Shaikhain,[1] south –east of the Uhud curve. It was there that he inspected the parade, and, as usual, rejected the too young or otherwise unfit (*Sirah* of *al-Sha'miy in loco*). There was a considerable number of women volunteers, including 'A'ishah, the youthful wife of the Prophet, who nursed the wounded, brought water for the thirsty and rendered other sundry services, as is described at length by *al-Bukhariy* (56: 67). *Al-Zuhriy* reports the Medinite Muslims asked the Prophet whether they should not ask the Jews, their allies, to help in defence, and the Prophet replied, "We do not require that" (Hist. of Ibn Kathir, Vol. IV p. 14). Others reports say about six hundred Jews of the tribe of Banu Qainuqa', led by the notorious hypocrite Ibn Ubaiy, came to the help of the Prophet, but the Prophet said, "We do not require them; we do not take help of infidels against infidels" (*Ibn Sád*, II/I, pp. 27, 34; *Ibn Kathir*, Vol. IV, p. 22). This is rather strange, as the Banu Qainuqa' were already expelled; but we shall return to this later. Muslims volunteers numbered a thousand in all. Later a gang of about three hundred hypocrites, under the influence of Ibn Ubaiy, deserted at the last moment on a flimsy pretext; and it was only with seven hundred strong that the Prophet Muhammad went to oppose an enemy more than four times that number. Of these seven hundred, only one hundred had coats of mail (*al-Sha'miy, in loco*). According to one report, there were only two horses, one belonging to the Prophet

Muhammad and the other to Abu Burdah (*Ibn Sád*, II/I, p. 27). It is not clear whether al-Zubair al-Auwam, who opposed on horseback the enemy cavalry under Khalid, mounted that horse of the Prophet or had his own, and whether some more horses were not fetched by Muslim volunteers from their homes nearby, on seeing a strong detachment of enemy horses, and fought under al-Zubair (Tahariy, p. 139 ff).

As to the enemy, the quarter million *Dirhams* were not spent uselessly by the Quraishite. There were "paid mercenaries" of whom two thousand belonged to the single tribe of the Ahabish alone (*Sirah*, by Karamat 'Ali', p. 245), besides a considerable number of Bedouins from other tribes. The Quraishites mustered in all 3,000 combatants, including 700 with coats of mail and 200 on horses (*Ibn Hisham*, p. 561). The cavalry was posted as right and left wings, under two commanders (ibid).

The Prophet takes up his positions

On the first night after the arrival of the enemy, when the Prophet Muhammad was still in the city, the township was guarded by patrols, as also the house of the Prophet, the whole night (*Ibn Sád*, II/I p.26). After the assembly and inspection near the Twin Towers of Shaikhain, the Prophet spent the night in the open camp, and a guard of fifty strong under Muhammad Ibn Malsamah was entrusted with the task of patrolling around the camp the whole night (*Ibn Kathir*, Vol. IV, p. 27). Next morning the Prophet marched into the curve of Mount Uhud and took up his position, making the inner opening as his camp. He decided to fight in the outer curve, and accordingly made his dispositions. He appointed a batch of fifty archers to take up their positions on the 'Ainain Hill. These, in co-ordination with the small cavalry under al–Zuzair, were entrusted with the task of protecting the passage between Uhud and 'Ainain from being penetrated by the enemy from behind the main Muslim army (*Ibn Hisham*, p. 560).

The Muslim army filed with faces to the west, wherefrom the enemy was advancing. The archers thus guarded not only the back of the main Muslim army but also the Quraishite passage to the city of Medina. This explains the unusually strict order of the Prophet to the archers of 'Ainain not to leave their post without express orders, even when the vultures perch on the corpses of the Muslims.

Then the Prophet Muhammad, after finalizing his tour of inspection on horseback, alighted arranged on foot the rank and file of his small army, and dressed up the right and the left flank (*Ibn Sád,* II/I, p. 27). He is reported to have put on a double coat of mail (ibid; *Ibn Hisham,* p. 576; Mishkat citing *Abu Dawud, Ibn Majah* and *al-Bazzaz*). Another report says, he exchanged the coat of mail of Ka'b Ibn Malik with his own one (*Isti'ab,* No. 902), apparently for purposes of disguise and security on the day of battle.

The Quraishite, too, feared a night attack, and a guard under 'Ikrimah patrolled their camp during the night (*Ibn Kathir,* Vol. IV, p. 27). On the morning of the battle, they advanced with their main infantry as well as half their cavalry of one hundred horse under 'Ikrimah, towards the Prophet. Abu Sufyan was their commander-in-chief. Women with tambourines were inciting them to war and of their cavalry, under Khalid Ibn al-Walid, was to go round and attack the Muslims from behind.

A conjecture about the then configuration of the 'Ainain Hill

The distance between 'Ainain Hill and Mount Uhud is so great that an enemy cavalry detachment could easily penetrate without being touched by the volley of arrows of the Muslims archers on 'Ainain. The Muslim cavalry also was too few to stop the enemy detachment. This difficulty can now be removed only by conjecture. May be the slope at the base of Uhud was not so low thirteen hundred years ago as it is now, owing to numerous inundations of the Wadi Qanat–one of which had washed the tomb of Hamzah and necessitated the removal of his body from the original burying ground to the present one – and to quarrying of stones for building purposes.

The Wadi Qanat, which is a continuation of the Wadi Wajj of Ta'if, seems liable to great physical changes. In 1939 I did not notice any bridge over it east of 'Ainain Hill, yet in 1947 a very old bridge had come to light there owing to an inundation during the previous years. As to buildings, the huge mosque and tomb of Hamzah, razed to the ground since the departure of the Turks, numerous houses on the very 'Ainain Hill, dozens of government and private houses for police and others in the vicinity of the battlefield would require a considerable quantity of stone and earth. Otherwise, in ancient times the part of the slope between 'Ainain and Uhud must have been so high as to prevent passage of cavalry, which was obliged to cross nearer 'Ainain and thus become a target for the presence of two springs of fresh water, there may have been in those days one or more palm groves and gardens, with usual compound walls, occupying part of the passage now open. This is supported by some reports of the battle. Abu Dujanah's incident is well known: how the Prophet Muhammad offered his own sword to the best warrior, how several people including 'Umar and al-Zubair, were denied the honour, and how Abu Dujanah obtained it on the promise of fighting with it unto death.

Our historians (*Ibn Hisham*, p. 56; *Tahariy*, p. 1426) have recorded an improvised poem of Abu Dujanah, which he burst forth reciting with joy at the great honour, a couplet of which says :

"I am the person, who contracted with his Beloved
(Prophet)
While we were on the foot of the hill near the date-palm grove."

The action : the tactics and defeat of the enemy in the first phase of the battle

The Quraishites must have mainly come from the Zaghabah camp to Uhud directly and encountered the Muslims near the present westerly Cemetery of the Martyrs. But how did the cavalry under Khalid come behind the Muslims, east of 'Ainain? Had they come along with the main army and just separated from it a furlong before the battleground, made a detour and come out on the other side of 'Ainain Hill, there would have been no surprise for the Muslims who could have diverted part of their forces to meet the danger. Many people suppose that there is a passage from behind Mount Uhud, which leads directly into the inner opening where the Prophet Muhammad had camped and which is narrowly separated from the battleground. In 1932 and 1939 I wandered for hours and climbed the rocks, and am sure that there is no possibility whatsoever of the entrance of cavalry that way. In 1946-47, I circumambulated the whole mountain, and assured myself that the north of the mount is a solid and high way and there is no opening whatever to allow for the penetration of man, much less of horse. The only possibility is that the cavalry of Khalid galloped round the mountain from their camp, about ten kilometres, which is certainly not too much for horses, and came in time upon the other side of 'Ainain to try to attack the Muslims from their rear. The march of Khalid from the north of Uhud necessitated not more than about four kilometres in excess of his march, had he come along with the main army group of the Meccans. This is certainly not too much for a cavalry detachment on important duty. Otherwise it will be impossible to explain why 'Ainain is also called "Hill of the Archers", and that name is not given to some height of Uhud near the narrow passage joining the inner and outer openings in Uhud.

The first phase of the battle ended with the defeat of the Quraishite main army, or rather the vanguard only. The repeated onslaughts of Khalid's cavalry were also successfully repulsed by the archers conjointly with the Muslim horsemen. Everybody then busied himself in plundering whatever booty he could capture (*Ibn Hisham*, p. 569). The battle was not yet over when the Muslim archers deserted their post, in spite of the stern warning of their commander, to take part in the plundering, thinking that the battle was over. The commander of the archers was left with only seven or eight men. When the inveterate Khalid attempted again, and this time with easy success, to penetrate the battlefield from behind the Muslim army (*Ibn Hisham*, p. 570).

The Muslims were not prepared for this attack. They turned round to oppose the formidable charge of enemy horses; and when the retreating Quraishites found that there was no more pursuit, they, too, stopped and reformed. The Muslims were taken from two sides, and when an enemy archer shouted that he had killed the Prophet—apparently misled by the change of coat of mail which the Prophet Muhammad had effected—the Muslims despaired, and fled in every possible direction (*Ibn Hisham*, p. 570).

Seventy Muslims lost their lives; twenty-three of the enemy were killed, most of them apparently during the first phase of the battle (*Ibn Sád* and *Ibn Kathir*, etc., in loco).

The Prophet Muhammad is wounded and defended by his followers

Several minor incidents are to be noted.

During the two days the Prophet was still in Medina or in the assembly and parade ground, the prospective battlefield was infested by enemy scouts and sappers and miners. A Christian monk of Medina, Abu Amir al-Rahib, and migrated to Mecca and had contributed in inciting the people against the Muslims. He was in the Quraishite army, along with his fifty followers, at Uhud. It is recorded that this monk dug several pits in the prospective battlefield camouflaged them. It was in one of these that the Prophet fell during the last phase of the battle (*Ibn Hisham*, p. 572).

The ground of Uhud is stony. During the last phase, the enemy resorted to throwing stones upon the fleeing Muslims. If several received wounds in their back, the Prophet was hit in the face. The stone hurt his front teeth, and the iron rings of his coat of mail thrust deeply into his face and held so firmly that, when a companion tried to pull them out with the help of his teeth, he broke his teeth, yet could not extract the rings from the bone of the Prophet (*Ibn Hisham*, p. 571). Later the Prophet Muhammad made ablution for his daily prayer services in bandages for many days (*Sharh al-Siyar al-kabir*, by al-Sarakhsiy, Vol. I, p. 89).

A small band of the faithful bravely defended the Prophet Muhammad till the last, and many of them sacrificed their lives in the noble task. A woman volunteer was also included in this improvised bodyguard, and her exploits elicited praise and appreciation from the Prophet Muhammad (*Ibn Kathir*, Vol, IV, p. 34; *Ibn Hisham*, p. 873).

With the help of some of the faithful, the Prophet Muhammad succeeded in getting out of the pit, dug by the monk Abu 'Amir, in which he had fallen, and climbed to a cave in Mount Uhud (*Ibn Hisham*, pp. 572, 576). This is on the east side of the outer semi-circular opening in Uhud, and big enough for a man to lie down comfortably; and was also out of reach of enemy missiles.

When the Muslim resistance was broken, the enemy indulged in outrageous rejoicing. Hind, the wife of their commander-in-chief, Abu Sufyan, cut the belly of Hamzah's corpse (he was an uncle of the Prophet Muhammad), took out his liver and devoured it to satisfy her thirst for revenge for her father, who had fallen in Badr at the hands of the same Hamzah in single combat (*Ibn Hisham*, p. 581).

A Muslim woman on the battlefield snatches the fallen Muslim Flag and Raises it till the last

There were nobler incidents also. When during the first phase of the battle, several standard-bearers of the enemy fell one after another at the hands of the Muslims, and the enemy flag itself lay on the ground for long, nobody daring to raise it, it was a woman, 'Amrah Bint 'Alqamah the Harithite, who snatched it and raised it successfully till the last. This gave later a theme to the Muslim poet, Hassan Ibn Thabit, to compose a satire against the Ahabish who had come to the aid of the Quraish and had fled in the first phase, to wit:

"Had not the Harithite girl been there, they would have been

Sold in markets like slaves" (*Ibn Hisham*, p. 571).

A hypocrite utilized the opportunity of the Muslim defeat to kill a Muslim for private vengeance. Later he was tried, and when found guilty was sentenced to death by the Prophet (*Ibn Habib, al-Muhabbar*, p. 467; *Ibn Hisham*, p. 579).

Another Muslim was killed at the hands of the Muslims by mistake. Blood money could be imposed, yet the son of the deceased, Hudhaifah Ibn al-Yaman, waived his right "for the sake of God", in view of the peculiar circumstances (*Ibn Hisham*, pp. 577, 607). Possibly the poor old man forgot the watchword during the turmoil, and was not recognized by his comrades, since he was a latecomer in the field.

The End

Slowly the news of the safety of the Prophet spread, and the Muslims began to gather round him again. A party of the enemy wanted to climb to the cave, but the Muslims pelted them with stones from high, and their number must also have been considerable. The enemy also did not suspect that the Prophet was there. So they retired without much ado (*Ibn Hisham*, p. 576). The enemy chief, Abu Sufyan, after apparently giving orders to his army to retire to their camp, made a final round of the battlefield, and found out the fact about the Prophet Muhammad. He was shouting boastfully, and the Prophet asked his companions not to reply. Yet when Abu Sufyan uttered some insulting remarks about the Prophet Muhammad, the famous altercations passed between him and 'Umar, who was with the Prophet (*Ibn Hisham*, pp. 582-3 ; *Ibn Sád*, II/I, p. 33) :

"Raised be the idol Hubal.

God is the Highest and the most Majestic.

We have the idol 'Uzza which ye have not.

God is our Friend (*Mawla*), and not yours.

Tell me the truth, O "Umar, whether Ibn Qumai'ah is right in his claim of having killed Muhammad, for I trust you more than him.

O enemy of God, the Prophet and Abu Bakr are alive actually listen to what thou sayest.

Uhud for Badr, a day for a day.

Yes, but our martyrs are in paradise, and yours in hell."

The Quraishites had already retired to the camp, and their chief did not, or could not, recall his men to capture this last pocket of Muslim resistance. He followed suit.

The Prophet Muhammad was intrigued at their suspicious withdrawal. He concluded that they were going to sack the undefended city of Medina. So, in spite of wounds, he at once prepared as best he could to reorganize his handful of men for defence. Yet his intelligence service men soon brought the report that the enemy were riding their camels, and that the horses were being led alongside bare-backed. The Prophet said: "In that case, they are intending a long journey back home, and not any immediate warlike activity" (*Ibn Hisham*, p. 583).

The Prophet was still not satisfied. He thought, the enemy must very soon repent and return back to Medina in order to pursue his victory to the end. And he was right. Anyhow, the Prophet marched a considerable distance in the wake of the enemy, sent also some advanced scouts—two of whom were captured and murdered by the enemy (*Ibn Sád*, II/I, p. 35)—some of whom succeeded in assuring the enemy that the Prophet Muhammad had recovered and was prepared to meet them with a force stronger than the one he had mustered at Uhud; and the enemy's counter-bluff had no effect on the Muslims. The Prophet camped with the Muslims at Hamra al-Asad, about ten miles from Medina, on the Wadi al-'Aqiq, on the left of Dhu 'l-Hulaifah, and caused to be lit five hundred fires during the night (Ibid); and after several days, when there was no more possibility of the enemy's return, he marched back to Medina (*Ibn Hisham*, p. 588).

Ibn Sád (II/I, p. 34) assures us that on his return from Uhud, and before his march in the wake of the enemy, the Prophet had posted guards for the protection of the city of Medina. *Ibn Kathir* (Vol. IV, p. 20) describes in detail how the

Prophet at Uhud took his own position under the banner of the Ansarites, and how he issued orders to different commanders for moving in different directions to oppose the enemy.

II

Preliminary remarks

During the past few decades, methods and principles of warfare have changed, due to the phenomenal development of science, to such an extent that ancient campaigns, however epochmaking in their own time, now look like child's play. It is no more too much for the so-called Big Powers to mobilize nowadays by a single stroke of the pen armies of millions on either side. Armament has so greatly been transformed that the top secret deadly engines to our own younger days are more useful in museums than on the field of actual battle. On the administration side, the means of communication, information and transportation have undergone such a change in power, number and speed, that the work, which formerly took months, is now accomplished in hours or even minutes.

The layman might therefore be thinking that the description of the wars of yore, however important or captivating to an historian, had no practical military value in the changed circumstances. But no, the recruits and cadets, in Britain for instance, are still taught in their very first lesson that:

"It must be understood by all officers that the most important part of their individual training is the work they do by themselves... Military history must unquestionably have the most important place in such study as being the best means of learning the true meaning of the principles of war and their application, and of studying the preponderating part which human nature plays in all operations. ...Military history, as already statred, is of great importance in the instruction of officers. It is for this reason that a special campaign, or a special period of a campaign, is selected every year for general study during the individual training season.

"In the study of military history the object should be to derive from the records of the past campaigns lessons *applicable to the present. To read with a view to acquiring merely knowledge of historical events is of little value. The size of modern armies and their approved armaments and means of communication render many lessons of the past inapplicable to the present. But human nature and the underlying principles of war do no change, and it is for this reason that valuable lessons can be learned from EVEN THE MOST ANCIENT CAMPAIGNS" (War Office Training Regulations, pp. 23ff. London 1934).*

The Importance of the battles of the Prophet Muhammad to a military tactician

It is obvious that full use of the study of ancient campaigns can be made only when it is carefully scrutinized and when we find out how the commanders applied the principles and what were the results. The battles fought by Muhammad, the Prophet of Islam (peace be upon him!), are characteristic of the man, conspicuous, head and shoulders above many others, past or present. He had fought the enemy, often three times, and on some occasions even ten times, the number he could himself deploy, and he was practically always victorious. Again, his "empire", which commenced with a few streets of a small City-State, expanded at the average rate of 274 square miles daily; and after ten years of political activity, when he breathed his last, he was running over a million square miles. This area, as big as Europe minus Russia, and inhabited certainly by millions of people at that time, was conquered at a cost of barely 150 men killed on the battlefields[2] on the enemy side. Loss of Muslims was at the rate of one martyr a month for a period of ten years at an average. This respect of human blood is unequalled in the annals of man. Moreover, the firmness of occupation, the mental transformation of the conquered and their complete assimilation, and the production of such trained officers who in a bare fifteen years after the death of the leader delivered millions of square miles from *bellum omnium contra omnes* to enjoy the *pax Islamica* and to be ruled from Medina in three continents[3] — these and similar other phenomena arouse in us an intense curiosity to study the wars of the time of the Prophet. These wars of the Prophet had nothing in common, except the name, with our mundane wars, and we see in his wars the truth of his own saying: "I am the Prophet of Battle, I am the Prophet of Mercy."

Difficulties of the task of writing on the battlefields of the Prophet

The task, however, is not easy. Every civilized language of the world, besides the original source, Arabic, has produced more or less lengthy biographies of the man styled by the Qur'án as "A Mercy unto all nations", friendly as well as hostile. There is no dearth of data on his wars. Still, I have so far neither read nor heard anything about the description of his wars, not from the point of view of history but from that of the military science. To write on the wars of 1,300 odd years ago requires a knowledge of historical data as well as of military training. I am not a student of history, and have not had the good fortune of leading an army life, rejected as I was on physical grounds on my candidature for cadetship in the army. Yet it would be sheer waste of time to wait and pray for the coming of a qualified person combining both the capacities and being disposed to undertake the task. The data I have so far collected by reading and by thrice visiting the sites concerned is diffidently published here, not for the benefit of others but for inciting the interest, through a non-professional challenge, of those who could revise the data and could better the conclusions.

GENERAL SURVEY

The Rebuff of the Meccans and Ta'ifians to the efforts of the Prophet Muhammad at preaching the unity of God

It is commonly known that the Prophet of Islam began to preach his reaching of the unity of God in the city of Mecca[4] from the year 13 A.H.—610 C.E., for which he said he was called on by a Divine Revelation received in the cave of Hira. This call was, on the one hand, against a prevalent hereditary belief in idolatry, and on the other hand, to accept it meant the acceptance of its teacher as the leader. As this latter signified the transfer of chieftainship to a junior family, not only others but even the elder relatives of the Prophet Muhammad himself, of the family of the Banu Hashim, resented it vehemently. When the senior family in the city took to active opposition, the commonalty were forced, as everywhere, to do likewise even as grass and husk in the face of a strong wind.

The Prophet had concentrated all his time, effort and resources to the one object of furthering the reform movement. Yet in spite of the passing of eight to ten years, even the small town—as Mecca, his birthplace, was then—could not be rallied: on the contrary, the very life of the preacher fell into danger, so vehement was the opposition. His affectionate wife, Khadijah, and his uncle and protector, Abu Talib, both died about the same time, and this double loss brought great and unexpected difficulties. For the new head of the clan, his uncle Abu Lahab, who was antagonistic to the movement from the very beginning, began to reprimand him, and finally excommunicated and outlawed him. Muhammad had to leave the town and seek new protectors. The family of his maternal uncles, the Banu 'Abd Yalil (cf. Abu Nu'aim, *al-Muntaqa*, § 20, my own *MS*), lived in Ta'if. His younger uncle and intimate friend, 'Abbas, had considerable influence there on account of his banking and business, as *Ibn Hisham*[5] assures us. Moreover, it is not very far from Mecca, the distance, being about 50 miles. I myself started in 1939 on a donkey at 5 o'clock in the afternoon and reached the base of Mount Kara by midnight, and, resuming the uphill journey early next morning, reached Ta'if before midday. Camels, which follow the route of Ja'irranah, take two days to arrive. The new motor route is a bit longer, about 70 miles, and the post van conveyed me back to Mecca in about four hours, with all its halts. In fact Ta'if, which had the same attraction for Meccans, even in those days, as hill stations in Eastern summers have for us, attracted the Prophet Muhammad for entirely different reasons. He travelled there accompanied by a freed-slave and family servant of his, Zaid Ibn Harithah, and had, if not very high hopes at least a chance worth trying. Yet the relatives there proved worse than strangers. Ta'if was more materialistic than Mecca. Mecca was the sole market for the products of Ta'if, and during the hot seasons it benefited from the tourist traffic of rich Meccans, who frequented that hill station every year. Hence, perhaps, it could not afford to irritate or displease Mecca. Moreover, in preaching the religion of the unity of God, a messenger of His had in Ta'if also the same handicap as in Mecca: the local potentates saw therein a direct threat to their own power and prestige. The Prophet implored his maternal uncles there, though in vain, that they at least should not divulge the news of the mission on which he had come.

Ta'if even today preserves the gardens and other sites connected with the memorable visit of the Prophet Muhammad; the garden where he took refuge from mischievous street boys who chased and stoned him relentlessly, until both he and his servant bled with wounds. It is said the kind-hearted proprietor of the garden gave him shelter and feasted him with a bunch of grapes at the hand of a Christian slave of his, 'Addas by name. These gardens and farms are nowadays outside the walled town, in a south-west direction, along the river bed of the valley of Wajj. In 1939, the sites were commemorated by means of tiny mosques, now mostly in need of repair.

People assembled at the annual fairs held near Mecca turn a cold shoulder to the preaching of the Prophet Muhammad

The journey to Ta'if proved so utterly futile that it seemed preferable to the Prophet Muhammad to return to Mecca even though he was outlawed there. Reaching the outskirts of the city, he made several attempts to acquire the protection of some local non-Muslim personality. Ordinarily, no Arab would ever refuse such a request from anybody, even at the peril of his own life, yet the circumstances—demanded an extraordinarily noble character to acquiesce in this respect. In the third attempt at last he succeeded, and Mut'im Ibn 'Adiy and his sons escorted him safely first to the shrine of the Ka'bah, where he performed his prayer-service, and then to his house (*Ibn Hisham*, p. 273).[6] Apparently he had to promise in return that he would no more preach publicly in Mecca. A decade had now passed over his mission.

There was no restriction on his activity outside the town. The pre-Islamic institution of pilgrimage was there, as also the annual fairs of 'Ukaz, Majannah, Dhu '1-Majaz, etc., none very far from Mecca. The assembly of pilgrims in Mina, about two to three miles east of Mecca, was an open, though none-the-less difficult, field of action. So a few months after his return from Ta'if we find the Prophet Muhammad in the month of Dhu '1-Hijjah anno 3 A.H., presenting himself, in succession, to as many as fifteen different contingents of pilgrims, coming from the four corners of Arabia (cf. *Ibn Hisham*, pp. 282-3; *Ibn S'ad*, 1/1, 145; Abu Nu'aim, *al-Muntaqa*, folio 105-17, my *MS*). He, on the one hand, explained to them the principles and objects of his mission, and on the other requested them to accord him their protection and take him to their country wherefrom to continue his activities. He assured them finally that very soon the treasures of the Caesars and the Chosroes would be laid at the feet of those who followed him (*Ibn Hisham*, p. 278). It sounded all so ridiculous to them at that time. If one cut a sarcastic joke, another rebuked him outright, while yet another politely excused himself, saying that his people dared not court hostility to the Quraishite Meccans. What perseverance he had: one after another, he tried fifteen groups. Every time a Quraishite fanatic followed him and warned every tribal group of the futility of listening to a "lunatic sorcerer", who at the same time brought a challenge to the Meccans (*Ibn Hisham*, p. 282).

The site 'Aqabah and the Pact of 'Aqabah

Near the plain of Mina, there is on both sides of the road from Mecca a chain of hills rising like a continuous wall. When going from Mecca, just a furlong before crossing into Mina, there is in this mountainous wall a curve on the left side of the traveller, a curve in the from of an arch or a semi-circle, big enough to contain the Juma' Masjid of Delhi or St. Paul's of London. This place is called 'Aqabah—originally and more correctly "Near the 'Aqabah", since 'Aqabah literally means a mountain pass, an uphill passage between two parallel mountains, and early historians called it *'Ind al-'Aqabah.*

Inside the curve of 'Aqabah there is actually a big well, and agriculture thrives. The place where the Pact of 'Aqabah was concluded by the Prophet Muhammad is commemorated from ancient times by a mosque of medium size. That this is very old may be deduced from the fact that it preserves several inscriptions in Kufic. It had no roof even when I visited it last in 1947, only the four walls standing. The mosque is now called by the local people the *Masjid al-'Ashrab* (the Mosque of the Ten). There is, however, no doubt whatever that this is the mosque of the Pact of 'Aqabah, for the famous expert of the history of Mecca, Taqi al-Din al-Fasiy, in the third edition of his history of the holy city, *Tahsil al-Maram fi a Akhbar al-Balad al-haram* (MS. Qarawiyyin, Fes), writes:

> *"And the mosque of the Pact...This mosque lies close to the mountain pass ('Aqabah) of Mina: between it, i.e., the mosque and the 'Aqabah, there is a stone's throw or slightly more. It is on the left of one going (from Mecca) towards Mina. It was constructed in the year 144, and again in 629 by the Abbasid Caliph al-Mustansir, the former being constructed by al-Mansur."*

In short, this 'Aqabah curve is so big that twenty to fifty people can gather there without being noticed by passers-by. It was here that the Prophet Muhammad met five or six people from Medina. It is not clear whether they had camped there or had merely come there when Muhammad met them and addressed to them his message. This party heard the call of Islam and the Unity of god with interest, and unlike others, found it worthwhile to accept it and co-operate with the Prophet (*Ibn Hisham*, p. 286ff).

What was the reason for their sympathetic bent and mental difference from other Arabs? They were Medinites of the tribe of the Khazraj, to which the mother of the Prophet belonged (*Ibn Hisham*, p. 107). And she had paid a visit to them even when Muhammad, our Prophet, was a young boy, and she had stayed there long enough to enable the boy to learn" good swimming in the spacious well of the Banu al-Najjar" (*Sirah Sha'miyah*). Again, 'Abbas, the younger uncle of the Prophet, too, used to pass several days in Medina with this tribe every time he went to Syria or returned from there, in connection with his commerce (*Ibn Hisham*, p. 294), thus keeping the relationship alive. Moreover, these Medinites had relations of alliance with some of their local Jewish tribes and those of hostility with some others; and hence they must constantly have heard that the Jews awaited the arrival of a Prophet regarding whom the Jews asserted they would follow him and subdue under his leadership all their enemies (*Ibn Hisham*, p. 286). Why not follow the same promised prophet and steal a prior right to honours and victories? When 'Abd al-Muttalib, grandfather of the Prophet, and Naufal, the former's uncle, had provoked between themselves a serious quarrel in Mecca, the Khazrajites of Medina had rushed military aid in favour of 'Abd al-Muttalib (Tabariy, Hist., p. 1084-86). Possibly the Khazrajites now expected the help of the clan of the Prophet Muhammad against their cousins and erstwhile enemies, the Awsites of Medina.

Whatever the original reasons, the grace of God guided them, and their own reason and mental abilities prompted them to embrace Islam forthwith.

The feuds of the Arab tribes of Medina, the Awsites and the Khazrajites, had been responsible for much bloodshed for generations past. Both were exhausted now, and the saner members of either were prepared to end the hostilities and settle their relations at any cost (*Ibn Hisham*, p. 287). In view of their mutual jealousies and rivalries and *amour propre*, a non-Medinite, as a neutral, had obviously a greater chance of rallying them both and becoming the common superior and chieftain.

Islam begins to spread and the foundation stone of Islamic polity is laid

When the six converted Khazrajites returned home to Medina, and propagated their new faith, a number of others were soon persuaded to do likewise. The following year, during the same Hajj season, a dozen people, representing both the Awsites and the Khazrajites, including five persons of the previous year, met the Prophet Muhammad in the same 'Aqabah of mina during the moonlit nights of the Hajj, offering their allegiance as well as that of their families. The Prophet enjoined on them belief in the absolute Unity of God, moral uprightness and obedience to the Prophet in every good act (*Ma'ruf*) (*Ibn Hisham*, pp. 289, 305; *Ibn Hanbal*[7] III, p. 441).

The Prophet Muhammad thus became, by a sort of social contract, the chief and commander of at least twelve Medinite families. And at their own request, ordered a Muslim teacher from Mecca to accompany them and supervise missionary activity in Medina as well as teaching and training converts in the details of the religious practices of their new faith. (*Ibn Hisham*, p. 289). The missionary not only succeeded in a large measure, but also his tact and devotion to the cause cleared the way for the whole-hearted collaboration of the converts amongst each other, even from the factional groups of Aws and Khazraj, under the banner of Islam.

One more year passed, and in the year 1 B.H. the Medinite contingent of about 500 pilgrims included 73 Muslims, men as well as women. They had come, along with their teacher, personally to offer their homage to their beloved Prophet and to invite him to migrate to their oasis. Islam was still the religion of the minority among the Medinites, and the majority of the Medinite contingent of pilgrims had come to seek a military alliance with the general Quraishites of Mecca. It was late in the moonlit night when the Muslims of Medina slipped quietly one after another to assemble together in the same holy 'Aqabah. The Prophet also appeared there at the appointed hour, accompanied by his uncle, the worldly-wise 'Abbas. The Prophet explained to them what his mission stood for, and they in their turn proclaimed their belief in, and testified to the truth of, his mission. After that they invited him and his Meccan disciples (*Tafsir* of Tabariy, IX, p. 163) to migrate to Medina, assuring him that if he did so, "We shall protect you even as we protect our own families," and when it was told them that it might mean war with the whole world, they still continued firmly to stick to their resolve and protested that they would never go back on their pledge. The Prophet individually shook hands with them in pact, and said: "From now on I too belong to you: (your) blood is (my) blood and (your) remission is (my) remission" (*Ibn Hisham*, p. 297). Then he asked them to select their tribal chiefs, and approved the twelve names proposed by them for the twelve tribes (cf. op. cit. *Ibn Sa'd*).

This was the famous Pact of 'Aqabah which definitely laid the foundation stone of an Islamic polity, with men, territory and organization. Obviously, when the Quraish came to know of this pact, they resented it vehemently, and considered it a direct challenge to themselves and a league against them. The non-Muslim Medinite pilgrims, who did not know what had happened, tried to reassure them and denied all existence of a pact.

The growing strength of Islam irritates of Quraish of Mecca

The irritation of Quraishites was daily to increase when the Meccan Muslims secretly or openly began to migrate from their birthplace, and escape from the clutches of the Quraishite persecution.

The period the Truce of God (*Ashhur hurum*) was apparently utilized by the Meccan Muslims for quitting their homes and hearths unmolested. The Quraish took a very serious view of the migration of the Muslim population from Mecca and their concentration in Medina on the trade artery of the Quraishites, in spite of the fact that many members of the very family of the Prophet were staunch "Meccans", and would not leave the town; on the contrary, they held important positions in city councils, such as 'Abbas, who was the head of the sacred well of Zamzam, and Abu Lahab, who was the worst enemy of Islam. So the Quraishites hatched a dangerous conspiracy against the life of the Prophet Muhammad. Obviously this was the end of all peace or tolerance, and an unconcealed act of war against Islamdom (Ibn Hisham, p. 323ff).

The Prophet managed to leave his house while it was actually besieged by those who had come with the avowed intention of murdering him when he came out (*Ibn Hisham*, p. 323ff), left the township of Mecca, spent a couple of days in the cave of Thawr, until agitation subsided in the city, and finally set out for Medina early in the month of Rabi' I, by a route not commonly used, and reached his destination in about twelve nights' journey. The news of his "disappearance" had preceded him to Medina, and naturally people guessed his destination. After several days of anxious expectancy and disappointments, the people of Qubaa, a village south of Medina, espied one day from afar a small caravan of two camels plying in the host sun towards their township. They were not wrong this time, and the Prophet Muhammad, a slave servant of his, and Abu Bakr, were led by a hired guide. Words fail to describe the stir and joyous enthusiasm of the population at the arrival of the Prophet of God, and supreme head of their religion and their polity. Men and women, young and old, all put on their best attire and took their weapons and clustered on a prominent mound which is still commemorated as *Thaniya al-Wadd*, on the southern side of the city of Medina, in order to gaze down on him and receive him with a welcome unsurpassed in sincerity by any in human history. The girls chanted along with boys, beating tambourines and singing the following song of welcome:

> "The full moon has risen upon us
> From the Farewell-Hills.
> Thanks are incumbent upon us

> So long as a praying person prays to God.
> O thou, who hast been provoked among us,
> Thou hast brought a command which shall be obeyed."

Some Arab historians mention that while on his way to Medina the Prophet received Buraidah al-Aslamiy, along with several dozen of the latter's comrades, and that they escorted him with flowing banners and served him as a bodyguard (*Sirah Sha'miyah*). Curiously enough, there is no mention of them at the time of the arrival of the Prophet in Qubaa, as we have seen, in the outskirts of Medina. The Prophet must have permitted them to return after a few hours' journey in his company.

The Quraishites in Mecca were naturally very much annoyed at his successful escape, and as an immediate reaction confiscated the landed and other properties left behind by the Prophet and other emigrants (*Bukhariy*, 64: 84, No. 3; *Ibn Hisham*, pp. 321-22, 339; *Mubsut* of Sarakhsiy Vol. X, p. 52), The persecution of the few poor Muslims still remaining in Mecca was intensified.

The Prophet Muhammad's solution of the refugee problem. Some details of the first written Constitution of a State in the world

The tough time of real action was now beginning.

First, the Prophet caused a fraternization between Meccan refugees and the well-to-do Medinite Ansars of the tribes of Aws and Khazraj (*Ibn Hisham*, p. 344). This solved the problem of how to rehabilitate the uprooted. The principle of the fraternization was that the two contractual brothers should enjoy the property jointly, and the profit of the labours of both should also go to the common funds. So much so, that they inherited from each other to the exclusion of other customary kinsmen (*Tafsir* of Tabariy, under the Qur'ánic verse 8:75). The Government, too took notice of the fact, and was careful to enlist only one of the two contractual brothers while selecting volunteers to send on official expeditions, the other remaining at home and taking care of both families.

Thereafter the rights and duties of the ruler and the ruled were promulgated in a precise document, which constituted a federal City-State in the plain (*Jawf*) of Medina, and dealt with social insurance, administration of justice, foreign relations, defence and several other matters of central administration, including the detail of final authority resting with the Prophet Muhammad in case of disputes between individuals (*Ibn Hisham*, pp. 341-44; Abu 'Ubaid, Kitab al-Amwal, § 517; The Islamic Review, Woking, 1941, August to November). This was followed by a treaty or instrument of accession to the City-State so constituted on the part of the Jewish tribes inhabiting Medina. This treaty with the Jews dealt particularly with questions of military and political significance, and the Jews were also persuaded to acknowledge Muhammad (may peace abide with him!) as their supreme chief and common superior, as has been explicitly mentioned in the document. Like the Arabs of Medina, the Jews, too, were there split into warring factions, and the neutral personality of a third entity, who could administer impartial justice and restore peace and order in the city, was obviously not unwelcome to any of them. The treaty with the Jews and the regulation of the Medinite Muslims all were incorporated into a single Sahifah which in the words of Wellhausen (Gemeindeordnung von Medina) constituted a polity in the anarchic city. Fortunately, this document, the first written constitution of a State in the world, has been preserved verbatim and in toto by historians and has come down to us intact. This constitution endowed the conglomeration of Medina with a Haram, a sacred territory, a preserve, a political entity with definite territory, and a City-State with a constitution elastic enough to serve later greater needs when the city became a metropolis of a vast empire embracing the whole of Arabia in the very lifetime of the Prophet.

The Meaning of the word *Haram*

The term Haram requires, perhaps, some elucidation. It has a significance half-religious and half-political. We come across it in pre-Islamic days not only in different parts of

Arabia but also in Palestine, Greece and elsewhere. From the religious point of view, it signified that everything within its limits should be considered sacred: birds and beasts should not be hunted there; trees should not be hewn down; bloodshed should not be allowed; and the people coming there should on no account be molested in this general refuge, even if they were criminals sought after. Politically, Haram meant the determination of the territorial limits of the City-State. (I have contributed a separate monograph on the City-State of Mecca, detailing its political system in the Days of Ignorance, in the quarterly, Islamic Culture, Hyderabed-Deccan, 1938.) The pillars erected to delimit the Haram of Mecca are said to date from the days of Abraham (peace be with him!). Anyhow, they existed in pre-Islamic days. On the conquest of Mecca, in the year 8 A.H., the Prophet Muhammad renovated these constructions (cf. Mir at al-*Haramain,* 'Vol. I, *in loco*). Ever since they have been repaired whenever necessity arose.

In the constitution of the City-State of Medina, under review, Medina too has been declared a Haram. Incidentally, it may be mentioned that when Ta'if capitulated in 9 A.H., that city was also recognized as a Haram, as has been expressly mentioned in the pact concluded between the Prophet and the people of Ta'if (c.f. Abu *'Ubaid, Kitab al-Amwal,* § 506), and a special proclamation on the part of the Prophet Muhammad provided sanctions against its violation (for texts of both cf. my *Documents sur al Diplomatie Musulmane,* Nos. 160, 161; also Kanz al-'Ummal, Vol. II, No. 2132).

Had demarcating pillars been erected around Medina also? Al-Bukhariy precises only this, that the Prophet Muhammad sent a companion of his to erect such pillars on the limits of the city of Medina. General histories and books of Hadith refer to it by saying that the Haram of Medina was between the two Labahs or Harash, or else, between Thawr and 'Air. Now, Labah is an old Arabic word for lava, or even for the plain strewn with volcanic lava. Harrah, on the other hand, means the earth or stones burnt with the heat of the lava spreading around. There are two such plains, extending north-southwise, and the city of Medina is situated in between. Thus they call it Eastern and Western Labah or Harrah, indifferently. Thawr is a small mount in the north of the city, west of Mount Uhud, and 'Air is a bigger mountain in the south of the city.

Al-Matariy, who died in the middle of the 8th century A.H., has written an important history of the city of Medina, *al-Ta'rif bi ma ansat al-Hujrah min Ma'alim dar al-Hijrab* (MS the Shaikh al-Islam Library, Medina), which is constantly referred to by all later authors. He gives greater details, as under:

> *"It is reported by Ka'b Ibn Malik, who said: "The Prophet sent me to erect pillars on the prominences of the sacred territory (Haram) of Medina. So, I erected pillars on the prominences of Dhat al Jaish, on Mushairib, on the prominences of Makheed, on al-Hufayya, on Dhu 1-'Ushairah, and on Taim.*
>
> *"As to Dhat al-Jaish, it is the mountain path of the hill al-Hufayya, on the Mecca-Medina road. As to Mushairib, it is the mountain to the left of Dhat al-Jaish; between it and Khalaliq lies al-Dabu'ah. As to the prominence of Makheed, the mountains of Makheed are on the road to Syria. As to al-Hufayya, it is in al-Ghabah (the forest) north of Medina. As to Dhu '1-'Ushairah, it is a mountain path in al-Hufayya, and as to Taim, it is a mountain to the east of Medina.*
>
> *"All this seems to be a day's journey in length and as much in breadth...*
>
> *"Dhat al-Jaish is in the midst of al-Baida, and al-Baida is the place which faces the pilgrims, who after putting on the pilgrimage-dress (ihram) from Dhu '1-Hulaifah, ascends westwards."*

The learned traveller of Medina, and librarian of the Shaikh al-Islam Library there, Ibrahim Hamdi Kharputli, told me in 1939 that the ruins of these pillars were still to be found to the east of Medina, and rise about a foot and a half from the ground. As their renovation after the time of the Prophet is never mentioned, these ruins seem to belong to the sacred construction of the holy time of the Prophet Muhammad.

The founding of the City-State of Medina by the Prophet Muhammad

After this digression, we revert to the main theme. The first act of the Prophet Muhammad after the migration was to found the bases of a City-State in Medina. As soon as his hands were free, he bestowed his attention on the surrounding territories. A glance at the map of Arabia will show that if the Meccans wanted to go to Syria or Egypt, they had to pass along the coast near Medina. If the tribes inhabiting the territory between Medina and the port of Yanbu' could be rallied, the artery of the Meccan caravan communication could easily be rendered dangerous to use, if not actually barred. These tribes may or may not have been allies of the pre-Islamic Arabs (Ansars) of Medina. Anyhow, the Prophet either contracted new pacts, or revived old ones, with several of these tribes, and included therein articles for military aid (cf. for texts my *Documents sur la Diplomatie Musulmane,* Nos. 140-145).

Several months passed in organization and preparation. Thereafter small detachments began to be sent from Medina to harass Quraishite caravans (*Ibn S ád,* 2/1, pp. 2-7), and to bring home to them that to traverse the territory under Islamic influence, it would be necessary for them to get the good grace of the ruler of Medina, the Prophet Muhammad. The immediate reaction to this on the part of the Quraish was to force the route open. The struggle took the form of several bloody battles. It is an aspect of these very battles, that is, the fields where they were fought, which is our theme in the following articles.

III

Situation

As the Hedjaz, and Western Arabia in general, is a hilly country, valleys and mountain passes are the roads and means of communication, wider valleys are selected by caravans for their route. More difficult to traverse are the mountain passes, and they supplement the valley routes in time of need. In other words, there are always several ways and by-ways between any two places. Badr is no exception to this. The route used in the time of the Prophet Muhammad between

Mecca, Badr and Medina has since constantly been altered with changing conditions. When Islam expanded, the pilgrims to the holy shrines numbered hundreds of thousands during the season. Before the first world war, caravans of ten to fifteen thousand camels were an ordinary affair. Naturally, camping space, availability of drinking water, and other similar matters must have carried weight in the selection of new halting-place, and it was thus that the *Tariq Sultaniyah* (the Imperial Road) of the Turkish period came into being. Camels, though rarely used by pilgrims nowadays, still ply on this route. With Saudi modernism, motor cars have practically monopolized the Hajj traffic inside the Hedjaz. Their needs and requirements are entirely different. The route used by the Prophet in the much-publicized pilgrimage of al-Hudaibiyah differed naturally from that which he himself used at the time of the conquest of Mecca, when his aim was to take the Meccans unawares; and it differed also from the triumphal expedition of the Farewell Pilgrimage, when he addressed the assembly of one hundred and twenty thousand disciples. Ibn Hisham and others have noted the names of stations in these various expeditions.

Unlike the Turkish period, there is no regular pilgrim traffic nowadays to Badr owing to the peculiar dogmatic notions of the Sa'udi rulers. In many places there are sand dunes, so abhorred by automobiles.

On the Imperial Camel Road of the Tariq Sultaniyah, one coming from Medina turns at Musaijid to go to Badr. Some years ago, the Muslims of Hyderabad, India, donated enough to construct at this important junction several rest-houses for the pilgrims, and their white building are a feature of the landscape. Some of them were occupied on 1946 by police, others by a primary school and many pilgrims passed the night in thatched huts. After Musaijid one passes by Khaif, now a small village, yet its grand mosque and other ruined monuments indicate that it has had its day of grandeur. Thereafter one stops at al-Hamr'a, a small village. Then passing by al-Haskafiyah, one reaches Badr the following day. Coming from Mecca, one leaves the Imperial Road a little after Bi'r al-

Shaikh at Darb al-Ajiah, and reaches Badr after about ten hours' journey on a camel. The route between Badr and Medina is very pleasant. The land being more fertile: there are oases miles long, and especially between Badr and al-Hamra' there is a thick forest, called al-'Is—which may have been the locality al- 'Is so often mentioned in the expeditions of the time of the Prophet—and there is plenty of sweet water and pastures for big herds of camels, sheep and goats.

Modern Town of Badr

We need not occupy ourselves with the history of the township of Badr. Nowadays it is a large village. There are several hundred houses built of stone, called locally *Qasr*. There are two mosques: one for daily services, having a small minaret (*ma'dhana*) for calling to prayer, requiring repair; the other, indifferently called the Mosque of al-Ghamama, or of al-Arish, is the cathedral mosque for the weekly Friday service. This is an historic monument, as it erected on the spot where the Prophet Muhammad had built his observation hut at the time of the Battle of Badr. It is situated on a hillock wherefrom one has a commanding view of the plain below on which the famous battle was fought. Actually, however, the palm-groves of the date-trees and other garden plantations obstruct the views in that direction. The canal, which gradually rises from under the wells to the surface and irrigates the gardens, passes underneath both the mosques, and serves for ablution purposes. The oasis is several miles long, and produces vegetables also. There is a flourishing Friday market, where the Bedouins flock from considerable distances every week and sell or barter away the varied produce of their country, such as melted butter, hides, oil of the elder tree (bailsan), live-stock (camels, sheep, goats, and occasionally cows), woollen blankets, striped cloaks (*'aba*), etc. In pre-Islamic days there was also a big annual fair (*Tabariy*, pp. 1307, 1460), which lasted from the first to the eighth of the month of Dhu '1-Qa'da (*Ibn Sa'd*, Vol. II/I, p. 42). There must also have been an important idol temple. There are, of course, no traces of it now, yet coming from the direction of Bi'r al-Shaikh, just about a mile before Badr, there is a curious rock resembling a seated camel. In the days of ignorance anything was good enough to be an idol or a fetish; it is probable that this too was once worshipped.

Geographical and Topographical Details

Badr is plain, oval-shaped, about five and a half miles in length and about four miles in width, surrounded by high mountains. Roads to Mecca, Medina and Syria converge here from different directions. During the Turkish régime the Governor, the Sharif 'Abd al-Muttalib, had constructed a strong fortress in the midst of this palace, but in 1939 it was in a dilapidated condition. The ground is bestrewn either with pebbles or stones, but in the south-west the earth is soft, and in places driving sand had also accumulated even in the time of the Prophet. On the day of the Battle of Badr it had rained, and historians record that as a consequence the Quraishite camp had become a swamp, while the driving dust of the Muslim camp had hardened, to the joy of the Muslims (*Ibn Hisham*, p. 439). The soft earth has now developed into a prosperous oasis.

The mountains around Badr have different names. They include two barren white hills, made of accumulated sand, situated on the two sides of the valley, still called, as in the days of the revelation of the Qur'án, the nearer bank (al-'*Udwat al-dunya*) and the yonder bank (*al-'Udwat al-quswa* (The Qur'án, 8:41). In between these two there is a high mountain, which is now called Jabal Asfal (literally, *The Mountain Below*), as it was below, that is, behind this mountain that the Quraishite caravan of Abu Sufyan had stopped (cf. The Qur'án, *wa 'lRakb asfal minkum*. 8:41), and having by-passed Badr, the caravan had traveled all along the sea coast and thus escaped the ambush laid down by the Prophet, as we shall see later. Al-Waqidiy says (*al-Maghazi*, MS. British Museum, fol. 30b): "Badr is from the sea coast at the distance of a part of day's journey." From the summit of Mount Asfal one has a good glimpse of the Red Sea, may be a distance of ten to twelve miles, and surely camels cannot reach there in part of a day. Either the sea has receded or the author, al-Waqidiy, has only surmised.

Causes and background of the battle

On the one hand, the Quraishites had persecuted mercilessly their Meccan co-citizens for embracing the new religion of Islam and forced them to emigrate, confiscated the property of those who left the city (as mentioned above) and brought political pressure, though in vain, on the ruler and other influential people of the countries of their refuge: Abyssinia first, Medina later (Tabariy, *Hist.*, p. 1603; *Ibn Hisham*, p. 217; the *Musnad of Ibn Hanbal,* Vol. IV, p. 198; *Ibn Habib Muhabbar*, pp. 271-3), for extradition or repatriation. On the other hand, the Muslims were retaliating, from Medina after the migration, by bringing economic pressure and banning the passage of the Quraishite caravans from the territory under their control or influence on pain of plunder. These were sufficient causes to provoke aggressive war on the part of the Quraish.

The attacks on Quraishite caravans should not be considered as simple pillage. Neither were the Quraishites innocent nor the attackers private bands: a state of war was existing between two City States, and the right of belligerency includes damage to life, property and other interests of the enemy.

It is for this reason that I do not agree with those timid apologetics who try to find arguments for denying outright the very existence of the expeditions sent to harass and loot the Quraishite caravans. The late Professor Shibli, a famous Indian biographer of the Prophet Muhammad, has no doubt strengthened his position, at least as far as Badr is concerned, by referring to the very high contemporary evidence of the Qur'án (8: 6): "As if they were being driven to death visible", and maintaining that the Prophet had left, not for attacking the commercial caravan, but for opposing the Quraishite armed escort or contingent. Still, the very next verse of the Qur'án (8:7) reads: "And when He promised you one of the two bands that it should be yours, and ye longed that other than the armed one be yours"; and is clear enough to show that at the time the Muslims were not at all sure which of the two they would encounter, the caravan or the armed detachment. The chances were equal. The caravan consisted of a thousand camels and carried merchandise worth half a million drachmas (the *Maghazi* by *al-Waqidiy*, fol. 8a); the caravan had learnt that already at the time of its outward journey the Muslims had pursued it (*ibid.*, fol. 8b); and the Muslims were sure that the Meccans would leave no stone unturned to protect their caravan by mustering all the volunteer forces of their own as well as of their allies. Thus to go very far from Medina in the direction of Mecca appeared naturally to many as to be "driven to the mouth of death." They were not afraid of death. Their enthusiasm was such that, when the Prophet rejected 'Umar, a volunteer, as too young, the boy burst into such cries that the Prophet was forced to allow him to join. The boy's joy was unbounded, and his elder brother, Sa'd Ibn Abi Waqqa, helped him to put on his war kit (*Kanz al—'Ummal,* Vol. V, pp. 53-57).

The caravan coming from Syria could have been stopped by the Muslims west, or even north, of Medina. But in spite of the special spies sent by the Prophet of Syria, in the track of the caravan on its outward journey, in order to keep Medina informed of the movements of the homeward journey of the caravan (*Ibn Sa'd,* Vol. II/i. P. 6), there were no telegraph or other rapid means of communication in those days, information of a camel-caravan could be given by camle-riders only, and could reach Medina at the earliest only a couple of days or so in advance, and mobilization and march and search would also take several days even when the detachment dashed directly towards the coast in the west. Certainly a big caravan of a commercial nature was less mobile than a military detachment, yet the guides changed their routes between two stations at random; and to be on the safe side it was decided to move towards the south, in the direction of Mecca, to stop the caravan coming from Syria, which is in the north. There may have been other considerations: people in the south were already friendly and allies: not so in the north, and hence the former could be a help instead of a hindrance in stopping a caravan, whose stay is always a soured of considerable income to the local population. The terrain of Badr may also have been a recommendation for opportunities of hiding and laying ambush.

It was the fasting month of Ramadhan, and the season was very hot. After one or two days' march, the Prophet ordered his people to break their fast for the duration of the travel. When leaving Medina, a deputy was appointed to dispose of official business; Muslim volunteers of different origins formed themselves under their respective banners; and Qais al-Maziniy, of the Ansarites, was the commander of the important rear guard (*Tabariy*, p. 1299). An incident of military importance to note: it is recorded that *en route* to Badr (as also later during the expedition of the conquest of Mecca), the Prophet ordered that bells hung on the necks of camels, etc., should be removed, apparently as a precautionary measure for concealing, during the night marches, the army on the move (*Imta'* by Maqriziy Vol. I, p. 38).

Badr was near the sea coast. It was a big station, and caravans generally visited it, and the routes to Syria, Mecca and Medina also converged at this junction. In spite of all this the Prophet could not reach Badr more than a few hours in advance of the expected arrival of the caravan.

The Prophet must have come by an unknown route, as usual. On his way he constantly sent scouts (Tabariy, pp. 1299, 1303), and sometimes he himself did duty by leaving his troops and wandering in the valleys with one or two companions, sometimes with success and sometimes without. It was in one such wandering that he got some important news about the enemy from a Damrah Bedouin (*Ibn Kathir*, Vol. III; *Ibn Hisham, in loco*; *Tabariy*, p. 1302). The scouts sent on camels from the neighbourhood of Badr (*Tabariy*, p. 1305; Ibn Sa'd, Vol. II/i, p. 16). had penetrated into the very township of Badr, as if for drinking water from the well. They overheard two girls talking about the imminent arrival of the caravan and how one of them would repay the debt of the other from her earnings in connection with services to be rendered to the caravan. This was enough, and they dashed back to the camp, where it was decided to lay ambush for the caravan when it would be entering Badr from the narrow mountain pass in the north.

As we have seen, the caravan had learnt that on its outward journey, Muslims had vainly pursued it, even as six or seven other Meccan caravans previously. It was apprehensive in this danger zone of Muslim influence. Incidentally, we may mention that in pre-Islamic days the tribes of Ghifar were notorious for pillaging even the sacred camels of pilgrims and they also lived in the territory of Badr (cf. *Abu Dharr Ghifariy* by Manazir Ahsan Gilani, 2nd Edition, Karachi, p. 18, citing *Ibn Hajar*); and Abu Dharr al-Ghifariy, who had embraced Islam in Mecca at an early age, had been posted by the Prophet several years before to preach Islam in this locality (*idem*, pp. 75-84. citing *Muslim*, etc). We may conjecture that the energies of some of the converts could well have been directed in other, yet similar, channels of harassing the enemies of their new religion, to the woe of the Quraishite caravans. Naturally Abu Sufyan, the leader of the caravan, was apprehensive. So he bade a halt at the turn Badr-Human (*al-Sha'miy, Sirah*), and set out by himself to see if Badr was a safe plain to stay in or cross. It was the hot season and camels travelled by night only and camped during the day. It must have been very early in the morning that Abu Sufyan arrived at Badr, and it is by the well that there are always people to talk to. Abu Sufyan was an important person, and probably on learning of his arrival the Juhainite chieftain, Majdiy Ibn 'Amr, must have come out of his tent to meet and greet him (*Ibn Kathir*, Vol. III, p. 265). Majdiy lived near Yanbu', and his presence in Badr shows what importance he attached to the big caravan that was passing. Any how, these people of Badr had as yet no news of the Muslim army, and Majdiy told Abu Sufyan that, with the exception of the two camel-riders, who had just alighted at the well for drinking water, nothing suspicious had come to his knowledge. Abu Sufyan hurried to where the Muslim camel-riders had alighted, and following the footprints came to a place where there was fresh dung. He took a ball in his hand, broke it open, and on seeing date stones inside exclaimed, "By God! these are camels from Medina, as this cannot be the fodder of the local grazing camels, and surely these are the camels of Muhammad! Thereupon he hastened back to where the caravan was waiting, dispatched a message to Mecca for succour by a fast camel-rider, changed the route of the caravan, and instead of coming to Badr, continued on the sea coast and made a two-night journey at a stretch, and thus escaped from the Muslim onslaught, reaching Mecca safely (*Ibn Hisham*, p. 437). On the way he dispatched another emissary to Mecca saying he needed no more protection.

On the arrival of the first messenger at Mecca, who in the traditional manner climbed a hill-top completely naked and announced the evil news, this naturally caused umbrage and indignation, for there was not a single house in Mecca which had not got some proprietary interest or other in the caravan merchandise. They could not make long preparations, did not even wait for the arrival of their allies, the neighbouring Ahabish—which they later regretted—and with a thousand volunteers, including a hundred horsemen, immediately set out for Badr. They did not cancel the programme even on arrival of the second emissary of Abu Sufyan regarding the safety of the caravan. This shows that the route of the two, the caravan and the armed detachment, was not the same. The continued rush to Badr was meant probably to try to eradicate the menace once and for all.

This Meccan force must have taken at least a week to reach Badr. It may be asked, why did the Prophet Muhammad continue to stay in Badr so long even after the escape of the caravan, and not return to Medina, his base and stronghold? It may be suggested he wanted to utilize the opportunity of this journey in order to contact local tribes and to conclude pacts of friendship and alliance if possible, and thus extend his sphere of influence on the territory through which the Meccan caravans passes to and from Syria. A branch of the

Juhainite tribe was already rallied in the year 1 A.H., and history records (cf. *my Documents*) other alliances of the Banu Damrah, the Banu Mudlij, the Banu Zur'ah and the Banu al-Rab'ah in the year 2 A.H., some of which may have been concluded at this time. All these tribes lived between the Red Sea and Badr, the region through which the Meccan route to Syria passed.

Be that as it may, when the Prophet Muhammad was expecting to meet the caravan, he waited somewhere around the northern pass, and probably continued to stay there even afterwards. But when he received the news that the Meccan army was coming in great numbers, he decided to oppose it. Some of his officers knew the terrain better, and on their advice the Prophet moved to the south and tired to dominate the water supply there so that the enemy would be deprived of it (*Ibn Hisham*, p. 439).

The Meccan Quraishites had come with musical instruments and were in triumphal vein. The Muslims were short of everything, even transport, two or three sharing one camel. Yet their morale could be gauged from the following incident: a Yamanite, Hudhaifah Ibn al-Yaman, narrates: "I was not prevented from taking part in the Battle of Badr on the side of the Prophet except for the fact that when my father and I embraced Islam and passed through Mecca en route, we were detained by the Meccans. They suspected that we had embraced Islam and that we would take part in the war ahead. We assured them that we were going to Medina on our private vocations, and had no intention of joining the forces of Muhammad. On our taking oath they released us. We came to Badr and narrated the incident to the Prophet. He asked us to go to Medina and carry out the pledge, and said: 'God will help us against the Quraishites'" (*Kanz al-Ummal*. Vol. V, p. 5348).

Again, on arrival inside Badr, the Prophet roamed over the plain along with some of his officers, and confidently showed them the spot where the enemy chiefs would fall dead (*Tabariy*, p. 1288; *Ibn Hisham*, p. 435, etc.). Leaving the question of miraculous prediction, the Prophet must have guessed the appointment of various enemy chiefs according to their talents and capacities for various flanks and posts and arranged his own defences accordingly. History tells us that he took particular pains to find out the names of prominent chiefs who had come along with the enemy forces (*Tabariy*, p/ 1304).

As battles generally began early in the morning, a site was selected by the Prophet for massing the Muslim army in such a way that if and when the enemy advanced for battle, the rising sun would not shine in the eyes of the Muslims (the *Maghazi of al-Waqidiy*, fol. 15a).

Details of the terrain of Badr, as given by ancient historians, are not clear in all respects. It is possible that some physical changes have occurred during the last thirteen hundred odd years regarding, for instance, the water-course mentioned by them. However, actually there is an aqueduct, a sort of subterranean canal which flows from the town towards the 'Arish hill and thence towards the oasis, gradually rising in level until at a distance of about thirty feet from the mosque of the 'Arish it flows on the surface of the ground. As the mosque of al-'Arish is on the hill, it requires naturally some digging to utilize this aqueduct for its ablution cistern.

Probably the Prophet had moved from the "Nearer Bank" of the valley at the arrival of the enemy, and camped somewhere in the neighbourhood of the hill of al-'Arish. In order to cut the water from the enemy, who camped further to the south on the "Yonder Bank" of the valley, several big pits were dug and the water diverted to them not only to prevent it from flowing towards the enemy camp but also to store it and make it more readily available to the Muslims. It is reported that the Prophet lived in Badr in a "red tent" (*Kanz al-'Ummal*. Vol. V, p. 5256).

Story of the battle

Muslim volunteers were just over there hundred, and had two or three horses (*Ibn Sa'd*, Vol. II/I, pp. 6-7, 12, 15; *Tabariy*, pp. 1298, 1304). The intelligence service had learned from some enemy water carriers captured by Muslim patrols that the enemy numbered between nine hundred and one thousand (*Ibn Sa'd* Vol. II/I, p. 9). They had also one hundred horsemen, according to the same authority (p. 9). Without superior marshalling and generalship, this unequal struggle could not have lasted long. According to al-Tirmidhiy (cf.§ *Abwab al-Jihad*), arrangements for the deployment of the Muslim army were already finalized during the night previous to the battle. Early in the morning the Prophet arranged his small army in files and lines, and inspected them carefully to see if they were "as straight as an arrow." He had a baton in his hand, and wherever he found the volunteers not falling in a perfect line, he pushed them with his baton backward or pulled them forward (*Tabariy*, p. 1319; *Ibn Hisham*, p. 444). After that he nominated a commander for each flank. According to al-Waqidiy (*Maghazi*, fol. 15b), Abu Bakr was the commander of the right wing. But it is rather doubtful as Abu Bakr is reported by other chroniclers to have stayed all the time in the company of the Prophet in the observation hut. There is, however, a report, on the authority of 'Aliy, that on the day of Badr people took shelter behind the Prophet, for he was the most valiant soldier on that occasion (the *Sunan* of Nasa'iy). The Muslims were divided into three main groups: the Meccan migrants, the Awsites, and the Khazrajites from among the Medinites, each under a separate banner (*Tabariy*, p. 1297). Accordingly three watchwords for the day were also recorded (*Ibn Kathir*, Vol. III, p. 274). But as they did not number equally, it is probable that they were deployed in some divisions other than purely tribal ones.

The instructions of the Prophet to his army

After the arrangement of rank and file, the Prophet gave some important instructions to his men, who were the last batch on the surface of the earth who worshipped One God in the idolatrous and atheistic world of those days, and as the Prophet himself put it in his prayer on that day" "O God Almighty! help them; for if they are annihilated, Thou shalt no more be worshipped in future" (Ibn Hisham, p. 444). The enthusiasm of the idealistic Muslims must have been unbounded at the hearing of these compliments. The practical instructions, given by the Prophet, said" "Do not move to break your lines but stay on; do not commence fighting until I order; do not waste your arrows while the enemy is still beyond reach, discharge your arrows only when the target is within reach; when the enemy approaches, begin to throw stones with your hands; on his nearer approach use lances and spears, the sword being drawn only finally for hand-to-hand fighting" (*Ibn Hisham*, p. 443; *Bukhari, Abu Dawud*, etc., cited by the *Mishkat*). Every Muslim must have collected around him stones, the grenades of those days, in considerable number. That was practical only for the Muslims, who were on the defensive: the enemy, on the offensive, could not, even had they wished, have carried more than one or two stones each as they advanced from their base.

The famous dictum of the Prophet "God has prescribed to behave well in every matter; so, even when you kill, kill in a better way", has a moral and an aesthetic value of no mean order (*the Sahib* of Muslim, Vol. VI, p. 72). It was enjoined probably at this very occasion of Badr, the first battle in which the Prophet of Islam personally took part. Unnecessarily torturous ways of killing, the killing of women and children and those of the enemy personnel who do not actually fight, such as cooks, personal servants and the like, are expressly prohibited.

The Qur'án enjoins, in this connection of Badr, an interesting method of combat, and says (8: 12) "and smite them each joint." It was to render the enemy unable to fight any longer yet not necessarily fatal. In a hand-to-hand fight this would diminish bloodshed as much as possible, without defeating the purpose of war.

There was as yet no uniform dress among the Muslims, much less among the non-Muslims. So friends were generally distinguished from foes by the use of watchwords shouted on both sides at each single combat. According to al-Waqidiy (the *Maghazi*, fol. 6a): "O victorious, slay" (*Yamansur amit*) was the general watchword. According to Ibn Kathir (Vol. III, p. 274) "One God, One God" (*Ahad, Ahad*) was the general phrase, together with several others, to wit, "O cavalry of God" for horsemen, "*O Banu 'Abd al-Rahman*" for Meccan migrants, "*O Banu 'Abdallah*" for the Khazrajites, and "*O Banu' 'Ubaidallah*" for the Awsites. Be that as it may, the essential is to point out how friends were distinguished from the enemy in the fury of battle. Yet already there was a tendency to have uniform dress. The verses of the Qur'án revealed in connection with the Battle of Badr refer to "marking angels" (3: 125). Commenting on them, al-Tabariy in his Tafsir records that the Prophet had ordered on that occasion, "O Muslims, the angels God has sent for your help have distinctive marks; so have you also distinctive marks." And the author adds,"... those who could improvise put at once crests of wool on their helmets and caps" (the *Tafsir* by Tabariy, under verse 3: 125 *Kanz al-'Ummal,* Vol. V, p. 5349, etc.).

Not much is known of the enemy formation. According to al-Waqidiy (the *Maghazi*, fol. 15b), they had only two flanks, right and left. Yet according to the same source the army had curiously enough three banners. When advancing, they halted at a certain distance and, as usual in those days, challenged to individual combat (*Ibn Hisham*, p. 443ff).

The Prophet had spent the whole of the previous night in prayer to God. Now satisfied with the formation and other arrangements of his small army, he, along with his immediate "staff" mounted a hill from whence he had a commanding view of the field of battle. A hut had been constructed there with his permission, the famous '*arish*, partly to protect him from the hot sun and partly from stray enemy arrows. Some fast dromedaries were also posted there (*Ibn Hisham*, pp. 439-40). Certainly the chief commander could also serve for the escape of the high command if the battle ended unexpectedly. The route of Medina was open from this observation post. According to al-Tabariy (p. 1322) there was also a picked guard posted at this hut, arish. The hill 'Arish' now takes its name from this hut itself.

'Arish and graveyard visited

In later times this hut of the Prophet was commemorated by a mosque, which replaced it. In 1939 there was a cathedral mosque, though small, on the spot. It had three inscriptions, all in Arabic, one on the wall above the pulpit (*minbar*), another above the niche (*mihrab*), and the last stone was on the ground near the niche. This condition of the last inscription dated probably from some recent repair and restoration. The walls were covered with mud, and I could not discover if there were bricks inside. The basement, however, was of stones.

The inscription above the pulpit contains the name of Khush-Qadam, a Turco-Egyptian officer of the Mamluk dynasty. As every line has one or more orthographical mistakes, they may emanate from the self-same non-Arabs. I have given the text in my *'Abd Nabawi Ke Maidan Jang*, and here I content myself only with its translation:

Line 1: "With the Name of God, the Beneficent, the Merciful."

Line 2: "The erection of the enclosure of this sacred place was undertaken."

Line 3: "By Khush-Qadam, decurion of the Egyptian State and constructor of the State building."

Line 4: "The completion of this auspicious building was achieved on 21 Rabi" al-awwal in the year 906."

So it is from the early tenth century of the Hegira. The other above the niche is inscribed in the Tughra style, and I was unable to decipher it, nor was there enough light to photograph it. However, this much can be recorded: it is in marble, and about eight inches square. The third inscription is on a small piece of sandstone, in very bad, yet orthographically more correct, handwriting, and it also speaks of a reconstruction, as the words Kana 'l-faragh would indicate.

The graveyard of the martyrs is enclosed in a special cemetery. During the Ottoman regime, marble pillars and inscriptions with exquisite workmanship were erected to make it a most beautiful edifice. Now there remains nothing but broken pieces of marble here and there. The whole thing is a pathetic ruin.

The guides also say that the battle raged on the very spot where the graveyard of the martyrs now exists. This may well be true on account of the famous dictum of the Prophet: "Bury the martyrs where they fell!"

The result of the battle is well-known. It was all over in a few hours. Fourteen Muslims lost their lives, but not before killing as many as seventy of their opponents and also capturing another seventy (*Ibn Hisham,* pp. 506-513). The prisoners were also treated in an exemplary manner in spite of the fact that the Muslims had least to favour them. The Prophet distributed them among his soldiery for safe custody, and enjoined them expressly to treat them well (*Bukhari* 56: 42). The command did not remain unheeded: those of the prisoners who had no clothes were provided with dress, and they were fed on a par with the Muslims. Some of the Muslims fed them with their bread and contented themselves with mere dates in view of the good treatment enjoined (*Tabariy,* p. 1337; *Ibn Hisham,* pp. 459-60; *Ibn Sa'd,* Vol. II/I, p. 111). According to the Qur-án (76: 8-9), feeding the prisoners is to be gratis.

There was no uniform treatment of prisoners of war in pre-Islamic Arabia: sometimes they were killed, sometimes enslaved, particularly women and young children, and sometimes liberated gratis or on payment of ransom or in exchange for somebody in the hands of the enemy. Ransom was in vogue in Islam even from pre-Badr days. Now, after marching for one or two days towards Medina and entering Islamic territory, the Prophet held a council, and in spite of tempting reasons to kill them all, it was decided to liberate them on payment of ransom. Four thousand drachmas was fixed as the rate for ordinary prisoners (*Ibn Hisham,* p. 462). Even the relatives of the Prophet were not exempted. 'Abbas, the uncle of the Prophet, certainly deserved better, for he used always to serve in Mecca as a secret agent of Islam, and constantly kept the Prophet informed of the local news. Yet he too had to pay. A cousin of the Prophet, Naufal Ibn al-

Harith Ibn 'Abd al-Muttalib, who was an armament merchant, was asked to supply one thousand spears as his ransom (*Ibn Hajar, isabah,* No. 8336). Another tradition relates that the prisoners of Arab origin were charged with forty ounces of silver (each ounce weighing forty dirham), yet the prisoners of non-Arab origin (Negroes) were charged only half as much (*Kanz al-'Ummal,* Vol. V, p. 5367). In spite of all this, what a pleasant shock to learn that the Prophet asked the literate among the prisoners only to teach ten Muslim boys each how to read and write, and this would be their ransom (*Ibn Sa'd,* Vol. II/i, pp. 14, 17; *Ibn Hanbal,* Vol. I, p. 246). A few were released for their poverty on promising not to come to fight Muslims in future (*Tabariy,* pp, 1342-54; *Ibn Hisham,* p. 471). There was enough booty (*Ibn Sa'd* Vol. II/i, p. 13), so the prisoners were not required to march on foot to Medina on the four-day journey.

All the dead, both Muslim and enemy, were given burial. Mutilation or any other dishonour to the enemy dead was strictly prohibited.

The Prophet sent at once two messengers on fast camels to Medina, one to 'Aliyah, the high town, and one to Safilah, the low town, to take the good tidings of the great victory (*Ibn Hisham,* p. 457). For many it was in fact too good to be true.

The entry of the triumphant army need not detain us. The rejoicing must have been sober yet very great.

International reaction was also not lacing. It is related that when news of the Muslim victory reached the Negus of Abyssinia through some travelers, he rejoiced greatly, so amicable were his relations with the Prophet owing to the behaviour of Muslim refugees there, who were the ambassadors of their State and their faith (*Ibn Kathir,* Vol. III, p. 307). Probably this is part of the same narration recorded by al-Sha'miy (in his Sirah, § Badr), which reports that after the defeat of Badr, the Meccans sent two emissaries to Abyssinia in order to ask the Negus to extradite the Muslim refugees in his territory. On learning the move, probably through his secret agent in Mecca, the prophet, too, sent a special envoy, 'Amr Ibn Umaiyah (of the tribe of Damrah), who had not yet embraced Islam, to Abyssinia in order to counter in mischievous move of the Quraishites. As is well known, the Negus denied the Meccans their request for the extradition of the Muslims (*Ibn Hisham*, p. 716ff).

References

1. This place is commemorated now by the Mosque of Shaikhain, which is unique in the vicinity inasmuch as it has a roof with two domes.
2. This excludes the application of the law of the Bible of Jews of Banu Quraizah, at the award of the arbitrator of their own choice, after their surrender.
3. That is, Europe, Asia and Africa. According to Tabariy (*Annales, Vol. I, p. 2812*), it was in the year 27 A.H., under the third orthodox Caliph, 'Uthman, that the Muslim armies entered Andalus (Spain), and stayed there even when reinforcements discounted and they were cut off from all help from the home country. Tariq did not land on Gibraltar until 65 years later. Gibbon (*Decline and Fall of the Roman Empire*, Vo. V, p. 555), too, has a vague idea of the fact.
4. For the politico-social life in that time, of article "City State of Mecca" in the quarterly, *Islamic Culture*, Hyderabad-Deccan India, 1938.
5. Page 273, References to this book are from the European edition.
6. Page 273. References to this book are from the European editions.
7. References are to the first edition.

[***By:*** *—Dr. M. Hamidullah, Ph.D. (Bonn), D.Litt. (Paris)*

Source: *The Islamic Review & Arab Affairs, November 1952.*]

13

The Text of the Prophet Muhammad's Historic Farewell Pilgrimage Address

The Address lays emphasis more than anything else on social service and obligations of one individual to another, i.e., on cultivating social conscience

The Prophet Muhammad's Farewell Pilgrimage Address

The Prophet Muhammad during his Farewell Pilgrimage gave a sermon which could be styled the "Manifesto of World Peace". The Prophet attached so much importance to this Manifesto that he repeated it five times during that Hajj season! Once he gave this sermon on 7th Dhú-al-Hijjah in the second Sacred mosque at Mecca and twice at 'Arafát on 9th Dhú-al-Hijjah and again twice at Miná on 10th and 11th Dhú-al-Hijjah (11th and 12th) each day once.

Ya'qúbí, the historian, records that the sermon of the 7th Dhú-al-Hijjah was delivered by the Prophet while on a camel after the afternoon prayer and the sermon on 9th Dhú-al-Hijjah in the valley of 'Arafát in the afternoon first before the afternoon prayer and again after finishing the afternoon prayer; on both these latter occasions he spoke on camel-back. The sermon at Miná was delivered after the morning prayer, also on camel-back. His companion, Bilál was in attendance, holding the camel reins. On all these occasions the Prophet had a crier to repeat his words, sentence by sentence, after him. During the Miná sermon it was his son-in-law, 'Alí, who acted as the crier, while on other occasions it was a young man of vigorous voice named Rabí'ah Ibn Khalaf. The Prophet Muhammad had him standing very close to him and asked him to repeat after him each sentence.

When the Prophet Muhammad reached "Arafah (near Mecca), he asked Rabí'ah Ibn Khalaf, who had a very powerful voice, to act as crier.

During the Farewell Pilgrimage of 632 C.E. there were present at 'Arafát between 120 and 140 thousand men and women. The Prophet Muhammad repeated his sermon again and again because everybody could not make it convenient to attend only one assembly. As the pilgrims' presence in the plain of 'Arafát forms an integral part of the pilgrimage rites and his stay at 'Arafát is obligatory, the Prophet soon after the whole congregation was ready to perform the afternoon prayer mounted his camel. After praising and glorifying God, the Prophet said to Rabí'ah, "Say to them: O people! The Messenger of God says:

"I man a man like unto you. It is possible that you may not see me again in this place (the Prophet passed away about three months later—8th June 632 C.E.). Therefore listen to what I am saying to you very carefully and take these words to those who could not be present here today.

May god bless the person who, after having heard me, guards my words and takes them to others! It is possible that you do not understand the import of my words here, but there are people in the world who would understand the meaning of my words better than you. Therefore understand that you should take my words to others who are not present here today, for it happens often that the messenger does not know the importance of the message he is carrying."

When the Prophet Muhammad had finished his sentence and his crier Rabí'ah had repeated it, the Prophet Muhammad stopped and asked the audience if it had heard his words well. When every one shouted to say that they had heard them, the Prophet turned his face upwards and said "O God! Thou art my witness. I have conveyed. Thy message."

The Prophet said to Rabí'ah, "Say to them: O people. Do you know what month this is?" They said: It is the sacred month of Dhú-al-Hijjah.

Then the Prophet said to the Rabí'ah, "Say to them: God has hallowed your blood and your property like the sanctity of this month until you meet your Lord."

Then the Prophet said to Rabí'ah, "Say to them: Do you know what territory this is?" and they said: The Holy Land (of Mecca).

And then the Prophet said to Rabí'ah to say to them: "God has hallowed your blood and your property like the sanctity of this land until you meet your Lord."

Then the Prophet said to Rabí'ah, "Say to the people: Do you know what day this is?" And they said: The day of the great Hajj.

And then the Prophet Muhammad said to Rabí'ah to say to them: "God has made sacred and inviolable the life and the property of each of you unto the other like this day of the Hajj until you meet your Lord.

"The Lord has ordained to every main the share of his inheritance. A testament is not lawful to the detriment of heirs.

"The child belongs to the parent, and for the violator of wedlock a stone.

"You are about to meet your Lord Who will ask you to account for your actions. He who has a pledge should return it to him who entrusted it to him.

"This day all sums of interest are remitted, including that of my uncle, 'Abbás Ibn 'Abd al-Muttalib. This day retaliation for all murders committed in the days of paganism (the Jáhiliyyah) is prohibited, and foremost of all, the murder of Rabí'ah Ibn Hárith is forgiven.

"O people! You have certain rights over your wives, and so have your wives over you. They are the trust of God in your hands. So you must treat them with all kindness. You have taken only as a trust from God, and you have the enjoyment of their persons by the words of God.

"And as regards your slaves, see that you give them to eat of what you yourselves eat, and clothe them with what you clothe yourselves. If they commit a fault which you are not inclined to forgive, then part with them; for they are the servants of the Lord, and they are not to be harshly treated.

"And keep always faithful to the trust reposed in you and avoids sins.

"All men from Adam and Eve. An Arab has no superiority over a non-Arab; also a non-Arab has no superiority over an Arab, except by good actions.

"O people! Listen to what I have to say and take it to heart. You must know that every Muslim is the brother of another Muslim (and as he pronounced these words he raised his arms aloft and placed the fore-finger of one hand on the fore-finger of the other). You are all equal. (You enjoy your equal rights and have similar obligations.) You are all members of one brotherhood. It is forbidden for any one of you to take from his brother save what the latter should willingly give.

"Guard yourselves from committing injustices."

The Prophet then proceeded to recite the 36th and 37th verses of the 9th chapter of the Holy Qur'án which abolish the terminal intercalation of the year, and fix the month of Pilgrimage to the changing seasons of the year.

> *He said: 'verily, the number of the months with God is twelve months (in a year, so ordained by Him the day He created the heavens and the earth. Of them four are sacred, three consecutive and the Rajab of Mudar, which is between Jamádá and Sha'bán). That is the true religion. So wrong not yourselves.*
>
> *'Verily the transposing (of a prohibited month) is an addition to unbelief. The unbelievers are led to wrong thereby; for they make it lawful one year, and forbidden another year, that they may equalize the number of months which God has forbidden and make such forbidden ones lawful.'*

"And now on this very day has time performed its cycle and as it was on the day that God created the heavens and the earth.

"O people! Truly Satan has despaired of being worshipped in your hand for ever. But should you obey him in some matter which may seem to be trifling, it will be a matter of pleasure for him. So you must beware of him in the matter of your faith.

"Let him that is present tell it to him that is absent. Haply he who shall be told may remember that who has heard it.

"O people! So understand my words. I have left with you something which, if you hold fast to it, you will never fall into error—a plain indication. The Book of God and the practice of His Prophet. So give good heed to what I say."

Then the Prophet looking up to heaven cried at the top of his voice, "O Lord! I have delivered Thy message." And the valley resounded with the reply from the myriads of human throats with one accord, "And that thou hast!"

Thereupon the Prophet said, "O Lord! I beseech Thee! bear Thou witness unto it."

An Analysis of the Prophet's Farewell Address

In the Farewell Pilgrimage Address of the Prophet there are fifteen items which taken collectively could be styled "The Manifesto of World Peace". In this sermon the one thing which catches one's eye is that the Prophet not even once mentioned the importance of rituals—the prayers, the *zakáh* and fasting—and that whatever he said and emphasized had a bearing on human relationship tending to establish peace amongst men and security in the world. Ritualism is given no pride of place in this Address. There are fifteen items in the Manifesto. They are:

1. *The blood, property and honour of Muslims is sacred to one another.* In this regard the Prophet Muhammad said, "O men! Listen to my words and take them to heart. Know that every Muslims is a brother to every other Muslim, and that you are now one brotherhood. It is not legitimate for any one of you, therefore, to appropriate to himself anything that belongs to his brother unless it is willingly given to him by his brother."

2. *Equality of rights.* In this regard the Prophet said: "All men are from Adam and Eve. An Arab has no superiority over a non-Arab; also a non-Arab has no superiority over an Arab, except by good actions."
3. *The abolition of family distinctions.* He said that people should not take pride in their genealogy. It is the good actions alone they should take pride in.
4. *Interdiction of bloodshed resulting from old feuds.* The Prophet said, "blood feuds of the pre-Islamic days are under my feet, i.e., forbidden."
5. *Interdiction of usury.* The Prophet said: "All usury money chargeable from the pre-Islamic period is under my feet (i.e. cancelled), and the first usury money which I cancel is the money that belonged to my uncle 'Abbás Ibn Muttalib."
6. *The enforcement of the law of cease-fire.* The Prophet emphasized the importance of observing peace and the cease-fire during the four sacred months of the Arab calendar. The meaning underlying this observance of the sanctity of the four scared months was that the elders and leaders of the Arab community would thus be able to consolidate peace.
7. *Safeguarding of the rights of women.*
8. Safeguarding of the rights of the slaves, who, the Prophet emphasised, should be looked after in the same way as one did after oneself.
9. *The brotherhood of Muslims.* The Prophet pointed out that Muslims were brethren to each other and that they should each one of them respect the rights and privileges of each other: they should not backbite, and they should safeguard the property and life of one another.
10. He said, "from the sacred Ka'bah, as a result of the promulgation of the doctrine of the Oneness of God, Satan has departed; but do remember that it may try to come through other ways. Be prepared, therefore, to forestall its moves and machinations."

11. *The Prophet Muhammad anathematized transgression in any form or shape.* He said that the worst enemy of God was he who struck someone who had not struck him.
12. The Prophet Muhammad said that those who took pride in affiliating themselves to others who were not their and those who do not pay the full price of the work done by a workman were far removed from the mercy of God.
13. The Prophet emphasised that Muslims should try to effect peace between two fighting Muslim factions.
14. The Prophet said, "I am leaving beḥind with you two things which will bring you salvation—one of the Qur'án, the second my ways."
15. All men are jointly responsible about God's commandment and for the propagation of the Manifesto. The Prophet said, "Those who hear this Manifesto should covey it to others who are ignorant of it."

[***Source:*** *The Islamic Review & Arab Affairs, November 1969.*]

INDEX

N

O

P

❑❑❑